Savior, Like A Shepherd Lead Us

Joe Evans

Savior, Like A Shepherd Lead Us

ISBN: Softcover 978-1-955581-37-0

Copyright © 2022 by Joe Evans

All rights reserved. No part of this book may be reproduced or transmitted in any form or by any means, electronic or mechanical, including photocopying, recording, or by any information storage and retrieval system, without permission in writing from the publisher.

Cover Art: "The Shepherd," by Sir William Blake (1757-1827). Public Domain.

Parson's Porch Books is an imprint of Parson's Porch & Company (PP&C) in Cleveland, Tennessee. PP&C is an innovative organization which raises money by publishing books of noted authors, representing all genres. Its face and voice is **David Russell Tullock** (dtullock@parsonsporch.com).

Parson's Porch & Company *turns books into bread & milk* by sharing its profits with the poor.

www.parsonsporch.com

Savior, Like A Shepherd Lead Us

This book is dedicated to my grandfather, Joe Bivens, who changed my life for the better in more ways than I'll ever know and in more ways than I ever thanked him for.

Contents

The Cost of Discipleship is a Pound of Bacon...13
    Psalm 89:1-4 and Mark 5:1-20

Know Thyself...17
    Psalm 122 and Mark 6:1-29

Saying Goodbye to Traditions..22
    Psalm 51:1-3, 6-7 and Mark 7: 1-23

Pushing the Date Back 29
    Romans 8: 26-39 and Genesis 29: 15-28

The Dreamer Had It Right 34
    Romans 10: 5-15 and Genesis 37: 1-5 and 12-28

They Didn't Get What They Deserved...39
    Romans 11: 1-2a, 29-32 and Genesis 45: 1-15

Say Her Name..44
    Romans 12: 1-8 and Exodus 1: 8 – 2: 10

Who Am I That I Should Go? 50
    Romans 12: 9-21 and Exodus 3: 1-15

History Repeats Itself, As Does Deliverance..55
    Romans 13: 8-14 and Exodus 12: 1-14

Do Not Be Afraid, Stand Firm, and See..60
    Romans 14: 7-12 and Exodus 14: 5-14

Who is Holding Up Your Arms?..65
    Philippians 2: 1-13 and Exodus 17: 1-13

The Golden Calf Takes and Takes and Takes 70
    Philippians 4: 1-9 and Exodus 32: 1-14

In the Cleft of the Rock 76
    1 Thessalonians 1: 1-10 and Exodus 33: 12-23

But You Shall Not Cross Over There...81
    1 Thessalonians 2: 1-8 and Deuteronomy 34: 1-12

Who Are These? 89
    1 John 3: 1-3 and Revelation 7: 9-17

When the Lights Go Out 94
    1 Thessalonians 4: 13-18 and Matthew 25: 1-13

Misjudging the Master 100
    1 Thessalonians 5: 1-11 and Matthew 25: 14-30

Let the Same Mind Be in You 105
    Ephesians 1: 15-23 and Matthew 25: 31-46

They Came Confessing Their Sins 109
    Isaiah 11: 1-9 and Mark 1: 1-8

What Child Is This? 114
    Ezra 3: 10-13 and Luke 1: 46-55

Surprised by a Fulfilled Prophecy 119
    Jeremiah 31: 31-34 and Luke 1: 67-80

Fear Not 127
    Isaiah 9: 2-7 and Luke 2: 1-20

Home By Another Road 131
    Matthew 2: 1-12

Here I Am, But Who Called Me? 135
    1 Samuel 3: 1-10 and John 1: 43-51

Dropping the Nets 139
    Jonah 3: 1-5, 10 and Mark 1: 14-20

As One Having Authority 144
    Deuteronomy 18: 15-20 and Mark 1: 21-28

One Foot in Front of the Other 151
    2nd Kings 2: 1-12 and Mark 9: 2-9

A Sermon for Ash Wednesday 156
    2nd Corinthians 5: 20b – 6:2

Divine Things and Human Things 160
    Genesis 17: 1-7, 15-16 and Mark 8: 31-38

Braid the Whip 165
    Malachi 3: 1-7 and John 2: 13-22

Step Into the Light 170
    Numbers 21: 4-9 and John 3: 1 21

Reverent Submission 175
    Hebrews 5: 5-10 and John 12: 20-36

He Entered Jerusalem 180
    Psalm 118: 1-2, 19-29, and Mark 11: 1-11

Let Us Be Glad and Rejoice in His Salvation 184
    Isaiah 25: 6-9 and John 20: 1-18

Why Are You Frightened? 188
    1 John 3: 1-7 and Luke 24: 36b-48

Savior, Like a Shepherd Lead Us 195
    John 10: 11-18 and 1 John 3: 16-24

There's a Difference Between Watching and Doing 200
    Deuteronomy 30: 11-20 and 1st John 5: 1-6

The Next Book 206
    Ephesians 1: 15-23 and Acts 1: 1-11

Too Light a Thing 211
    Isaiah 49: 1-7 and Acts 2: 1-21

A Few Sermons on Mark

Mark is the shortest Gospel out of the four that we read in our Bibles. Interestingly, despite its brevity, it's full of challenges and insights that can help us to see ourselves, our neighbors, and our God better.

I preached these sermons on passages from the Gospel of Mark as the COVID-19 pandemic continued. These sermons were preached on Thursday to just a handful of people who led and recorded the worship services with me. The full service was recorded after lunch. It was edited on Friday or Saturday to smooth out our mistakes, then launched on-line on Sunday mornings. This strange way of leading worship was more like making a TV show than what I had grown used to. It enabled me to stay home on Sundays, but I would have gladly traded that Sabbath rest to avoid preaching to a nearly empty room.

The Cost of Discipleship is a Pound of Bacon
Psalm 89:1-4 and Mark 5:1-20
Preached on July 5, 2020

One question rises above the others after reading this second Scripture lesson from the Gospel of Mark: the pigs, Jesus? Did you have to kill the pigs?

I love pretty much everything pig related. I love pork chops, pork BBQ, pork rinds, pork ribs, pork cracklings, pork chitlins, all kinds of ham, and any number of things cooked in pork fat. I can't imagine a pork product that I wouldn't eat. That may not be the most attractive quality about me, but it's true. In fact, there was a man I knew back in Tennessee where we lived named Ron Neil, who once introduced me as "his preacher who would eat a door if it was greasy enough," so in reading this passage from the Gospel of Mark, I'm struck by the cost of discipleship.

Certainly, I rejoice with the one man who was freed from his own personal hell. Still, I ask because we must ask: At what cost and at whose expense was he freed?

Consider the swineherds.

I can understand why they asked Jesus to "leave their neighborhood" after he liberated one man while compromising everyone else's way of life, yet this account from the Gospel of Mark shows us something important about our Lord that is in the fine print of all the songs we learned about Him back in Sunday school. At small tables in little wooden chairs, many of us were taught to sing songs that went like this:

Jesus loves me, this I know,

for the Bible tells me so.

Little ones to Him belong;

They are weak, but He is strong.

Do you know that one?

What they didn't tell us when they taught us to sing that song is that Jesus loves me, and Jesus loves you just as much, so if you are suffering, Jesus may do something which inconveniences me.

Jesus loves the little children, all the children of the world.

Red and yellow, black, and white,

They are precious in His sight,

Jesus loves the little children of the world.

Do you remember singing that one? I do. Consider the implications. If all are precious in his sight, but some are devalued in the sight of the world, something must change. Something must give. That's just the way it is, and if you haven't ever thought too much about it before, consider the pigs who weren't even slaughtered.

Did you notice that?

They just ran off into the ocean.

There was no BBQ dinner.

There was no lard rendered.

No hams were smoked.

No chitlins were creek washed or stump whipped (Do you have any idea what that means? That's a little Tennessee talk for you.), but back to the point: just off, into the ocean they went. These pigs and their precious flesh were wasted, like so much else that love might call us to let go of. These pigs are lost to the sea like so much else that had to die so that one of God's beloved might breathe free.

Now, let me turn my attention away from the pigs and toward the child of God. There's a lot about Him in this passage, even though Mark is this very short Gospel. Mark is the shortest of the four. It skips right over the whole Christmas story, which would have been at the beginning. At the end, whereas the other Gospels let us know a little more of how the story continues, it just ends once Jesus rises from the tomb. Despite everything else Mark skips, this Gospel writer describes the plight of the man who calls himself Legion as though he were not writing the cliff-notes version of Matthew's Gospel but were instead Charles Dickens writing *Great Expectations*. Listen to this level of detail. From Mark, we learn that:

- He lived among the tombs.

- No one could restrain him anymore, not even with a chain.

- He had often been restrained with shackles and chains, but the chains he wrenched apart.

- The shackles he broke in pieces.

- No one had the strength to subdue him.

- Night and day among the tombs and on the mountains, he was always howling and bruising himself with stones.

- "My name is Legion," he said to Jesus, "for we are many."

- Not one, but a legion of unclean spirits possessed this man.

Why does the author include all these details? It is because Jesus is always helping us to see.

On the other hand, all the time we are blind to the plight of our brothers and sisters. In every society, someone or some group of people ends up chained and dehumanized, living out of sight and out of mind, until someone or something opens enough eyes to the truth.

From the time of Pharaoh in Egypt, we know that the Hebrew people labored under harsh taskmasters, but Pharaoh's household didn't have to think too much about it. Others alive today remember how their grandmothers would not allow the name "Abraham Lincoln" to be spoken in their presence because when those enslaved were freed, their entire lives had to change, only President Lincoln once said that it was the hardship described by Harriet Beecher Stowe in *Uncle Tom's Cabin* that raised the conscience of the nation. What history tells us is that evil thrives when people are able to ignore the truth of their brother's suffering. Certainly, that's true today, as we turn a blind eye to all kinds of suffering that we'd never condone if it were happening to our sister, brother, mother, or father.

Take poverty for example.

You know there's poverty in Cobb County. I know it, only a person like me doesn't have to think too much about it until our church starts distributing free food and a line of hungry people shows up in our parking lot. Eleven hundred pounds of milk, chicken, produce, and canned goods were given out at our church by our youth group in addition to the 2,500 meals that went out that same week through the MUST Summer Lunch Program.

I got to be a part of it for the first time the week before last.

I was asking each car how many people are in their family because we wanted to give more food to a family of seven than to a family of four. I gave a number of tickets according to the number of family members. That was my job for the afternoon, which was the easiest job out there until it started to rain. Once it started to rain, everyone else could gather under the overhang to do their jobs. I had to stand out there getting a little wet. As it was raining, one woman rolled down her window. I asked her how many children were in her family. That was a hard question I had to ask because each time I heard the answer my eyes were opened to the reality of poverty right here in our neighborhood. This mother told me how many, then I gave her two tickets, and she offered me her umbrella.

It makes all the difference in the world when we start to see all people as people and empathize with their suffering. Now if we do that, if we see a man in the rain as our brother, we might lose an umbrella. We might end up losing some bacon, or some statues, or some money, or some privileges, but we have to get better at recognizing all we stand to gain when we're willing to let go of what we once thought was precious.

Among other things, my grandfather taught me that.

This week he died, so I've been thinking a lot about him. His death was a relief, in a sense, because death meant the end of this prolonged illness. He led a long, full life; still, I'm also very sad. He's always been there, and now he's not. In fact, he smoked for years, and then he quit when I was little. I asked him about it once, and he said, "Well, my daughter had a son, and I wanted to be alive to watch him grow up."

When you think like that, what are cigarettes?

What are umbrellas?

What are pigs?

What is privilege?

What is wealth?

What is anything, if in giving it up, we might better love someone?

When we gather around this communion table, we see such a profoundly different example to counter all the selfishness we're exposed to, for here we remember the One Who gave up everything – His body and His blood – because nothing is more important to Him than us.

As you gather around his table today, remember all those who have given of themselves for you. Remember all those, your mother, your grandfather, certainly your Lord, who would have given up, not a pound of bacon, but a pound of their own flesh to give you life.

Honor their love by following their example.

Honor your faith by thinking less of yourself and more of your neighbor.

By the way, someone once asked Him, "but who is my neighbor?"

Let us all show the world that we know the answer.

Amen.

Know Thyself
Psalm 122 and Mark 6:1-29
Preached on July 12, 2020

Just before sitting down to really study this passage from the Gospel of Mark, I was giving our children a lecture on self-esteem. Now that I'm home all the time, they suffer through a lot of my diatribes on any number of subjects. What inspired this one was *Hamilton*, the Broadway sensation now available on Disney-Plus. I was so excited about its premiere that we watched it the day it was released. It seemed like everyone was talking about it, and Sara was telling us how the creator and star, Lin-Manuel Miranda, was interviewed the same day by Terry Gross on National Public Radio.

"What was he like?" I asked.

"A little arrogant," she said.

You might say that he has a right to be. After all, the *Hamilton* soundtrack, which he wrote, has been listened to more than four billion times. In 2016, the play won the Pulitzer Prize as well as 16 Tony Awards, and Lin-Manuel Miranda not only wrote it all, but he stars in it, both singing and dancing. He's incredible, and the show is incredible. However, to Sara, the right thing to say after being interviewed by Terry Gross is, "It's truly been an honor," while Lin-Manuel Miranda ended the show by saying, "thanks, bye," which is the way you hang up the phone with a telemarketer and is not the way you leave a Terry Gross interview, so I understood why Sara thought he was arrogant, but our kids didn't.

"What is arrogant?" our children asked.

That's when I launched into my lecture. "Arrogance is thinking too highly of yourself. Arrogant people think they're more important or more wonderful than they actually are," I said. Then I nuanced this lecture they weren't paying any attention to by saying, "Thinking you're less important or less wonderful than you actually are can be just as bad. The best thing is having a good, solid understanding of yourself. That way, when you hear criticism, it doesn't crush you, though neither do you ignore it, thinking you're already perfect and can't improve. What life takes is not low or high self-esteem, but knowing yourself, and you two are both absolutely wonderful."

That was my speech.

Maybe they didn't hear it all; however, I hope they will sooner or later because I don't want them to let criticism or rejection crush them, nor do I want them to go foolishly through life as the presidents of their own fan clubs. What life demands is that we know ourselves well enough to keep going.

I remember well one teenage summer several years ago. My friend Dave Elliot and I decided to launch our own lawn service. We made flyers. It was very professional. We walked all around his neighborhood placing these flyers in everyone's mailbox. I remember his mother suggested we not put our names on the flyers for we didn't have the best reputation. We were mostly known as teenage vagrants, and we only got one inquiry. It was from Jim and Flora Speed. Our pastor and his wife called and asked us to watch the dog while they were out of town, which we did faithfully, I think. Regardless, this was a short-lived business venture. We never tried anything like that again. One customer didn't seem like success, so we quit trying.

You won't make it through life that way.

Those who learn from experience and persevere, on the other hand, will. Take, for example, Mormon missionaries. Do you remember back when Mitt Romney was running for president, and the news was so interested in Mormonism? I remember these great news stories on the religion. One person asked, "Why are Mormons so successful in business?" The expert, a member of The Church of Jesus Christ of Latter-day Saints himself, answered, "Well, if you have to leave home as a teenager and go knocking on dozens of doors a day, 99% of which were slammed in your face, you'd quickly learn what it takes to make it in this world."

In this lesson from the Gospel of Mark, Jesus tells his disciples to "get out there and keep going!" He sent them out two by two and gave them authority over the unclean spirits. He ordered them to take nothing for their journey except a staff: no bread, no bag, no money in their belts. He said to them, "Whenever you enter a house, stay there until you leave the place. If any place will not welcome you and they refuse to hear you, as you leave, shake off the dust that is on your feet as a testimony against them" and keep going.

That's what it takes.

You can't let the rejections keep you down.

You keep going.

You keep testifying.

You keep learning and getting better.

You keep doing good even if it seems like the evil in the world is going to drown it out.

That's true of Christian discipleship, and that's true of life.

This long reading from the Gospel of Mark started with Jesus in His hometown. They didn't listen to Him either. To them, He was just the carpenter's son; yet did He allow their perceptions of Him to diminish His self-perception? Did He rethink His mission or His ministry? Did He hear them and say to Himself, "You know what, maybe I'm not really the Son of God after all?"

No, He didn't.

That's not what Jesus did. That's what we do.

Jesus is different.

Jesus knows He's a prophet even if His hometown doesn't recognize it, but Herodias won't feel like a queen until John the Baptist is dead.

Our long, second Scripture lesson could be divided up into three acts, which work together to teach us an important lesson.

In the opening act, Jesus is rejected by the citizens of his hometown, and he speaks that noteworthy phrase: "Prophets are not without honor, except in their hometown." In act two, the twelve disciples are sent out to minister far and wide, and Jesus warns them not to let those who won't listen get them down. Then in act three, we see what happens to those who don't know themselves and who can't accept themselves just as they are, but instead entertain foolish dreams of grandiosity. In Herodias and King Herod, we see what happens to those who live and die according to public opinion. In them, we see what happens to those who make bad choices, then work to silence the critics rather than learn something.

For years now, we've been warned of the dangers of low self-esteem. Here in the Gospel of Mark, we see that one with a fragile sense of self, a bloated ego that can't handle criticism in a healthy way, is so dangerous a person as to have the head of her critic served on a platter. That's how dangerous a person who hides from the truth is. Herodias is dangerous because she must kill someone to be OK with herself.

Jesus isn't like that.

His hometown doesn't recognize Him for What and Who He is. That's OK. He tells his followers, "Don't expect everyone to listen to you. If they don't like what you have to say, keep going! Their reaction cannot nullify the truth that is within you." You see, Jesus is like John the Baptist, who speaks the truth, even though it might get him killed because if you don't stand for something, you'll fall for anything.

And you will.

John the Baptist always tells the truth. He can't help it. He's like your bathroom scale. According to Jenn Hobby, resident of Cobb County and featured personality on Star 94 FM, 76% of Americans have gained at least 16 pounds during the quarantine. Today, you stand on it, and it tells you how much you weigh. If you don't like what it has to say, you can kill your bathroom scale. That's what Herodias did, though killing your scale won't change your weight.

That's how the truth works.

We don't always like it, yet it's still the truth.

Likewise, I don't want the coronavirus to completely derail my life. I'm tired of it. Still, my options are to accept the limitations and precautions and get on with it or ignore everyone who tells me what I don't want to hear. However, ignoring the truth won't keep me from getting sick.

We're living in this very uncomfortable place right now.

Everything's hard.

Life is hard.

Everything has changed.

Life is changing.

What are we going to do about it?

I could tell you what Herodias would do, but what about Jesus?

Last week, our neighbors told us that every time they watch a livestreamed town hall meeting where the leaders are talking about all the changes that reopening demands, they play a drinking game. Every time someone says the word *pivot*, they take a drink.

The constant change and uncertainty are so overwhelming.

There's no question that the reality of our life currently is getting us all down; however, it can't keep us from living and moving and growing.

What the disciples learned as they went out into the world preaching the Gospel is that they didn't have to control every outcome.

They didn't have to convince every sinner.

They didn't have to win every soul.

They didn't have to know what was going to happen every step of the way.

You know why?

Because that's God's job.

Life today requires that we acknowledge Who is God and who is not.

What's required of us today is not high self-esteem so that we think we're the Queens of Israel or low self-esteem so that the weight of the world crushes us like bugs on the sole of my shoe. What we must possess today in this strange world is enough confidence to keep going and enough humility to let God work His purpose out. We don't have to do that for Him. We couldn't do it even if we tried.

Let us simply run the race set before us.

Let us walk without growing faint.

Let us trust Him with all our tomorrows.

Let us rejoice, also, in His provision while there is breath in our lungs to praise His name, for His hometown might have mistaken Him for a small-town boy, though I know Who He is. You know Who He is. He is almighty. He is redeeming this world even as we speak. He is standing in the breach and saving this world from sin, now and forevermore.

Trust in Him today, my friends, for He is worthy.

Amen.

Saying Goodbye to Traditions
Psalm 51:1-3, 6-7 and Mark 7: 1-23
Preached on July 18, 2020

In the midst of so much chaos, I've been finding a lot of comfort in food. Have you? Last Monday for dinner, we did something different. Having bought two whole catfish at Kroger, I breaded them with cornmeal and fried them. We're a chicken breast family, so catfish was a little out of the ordinary. However, something made me want to mix it up, even though I'd never fried catfish before. As a kid, I'd seen my grandmother do it, so I knew it could be done. We'd often spend weekends in one of the rental cabins at a place just north of Clayton called Andy's Trout Farm. Andy and his wife, Betty, who my grandmother knew, had two or three ponds filled with trout, and what we'd do is use one of their cane poles and fish.

It wasn't fishing, strictly speaking.

There wasn't much sport in it.

It was like there was more trout than water in those ponds, but it was a lot of fun for me, maybe not so much for the fish. According to my dad, we were all allowed to catch just one, as we had to pay by the pound. Sometimes, my grandmother would let me catch hers. Then, we'd carry the caught fish in our metal buckets back to Andy or Betty, who would clean them, and my grandmother would fry them up in a cast iron skillet back at the cabin that we'd rented.

That's as close to a recipe that I had to go on when frying our catfish last week, so I got out our cast iron skillet, filled it with oil, dredged the fish in our cornmeal, and fried our whole catfish until they were perfectly brown and crispy. My grandmother's been gone for years, though cooking this way made me think of her, which was wonderful and comforting.

That's the magic of food.

My brother recently wrote about it.

He reviewed a book of poetry for a literary journal. In his review, he said that this poet described food in such a way as to turn the everyday meal "into sacrament." Maybe you know what he's talking about. I do. The Pharisees were good about that, too.

The Pharisees ate in such a way that the three daily meals reminded them of Who God was and who they were. They never would have rushed through supper or eaten a meal in the car on the way to a meeting. There was no McDonald's drive-thru in ancient Israel. It would have gone out of business, for these holy people stopped everything to think about when the grain had been harvested, who raised the goat, and did the cook wash her hands before she fried it? It was all a way of worshiping God with each mouthful. They were doing more than filling their bellies, for they were connecting to something holy in each meal. Thinking of food this way, knowthat what Jesus said to those Pharisees and scribes must have been so completely destabilizing that they felt as though they'd been hit upside the head by a cast iron skillet.

They asked Him, "Why do your disciples not live according to the tradition of the elders, but eat with defiled hands?" Then He said to them, "You abandon the commandments of God and hold to human tradition."

Can you believe He said that?

Here's some advice: don't invite Jesus over for dinner unless you're ready.

He would have suggested that I grill my catfish, or worse. He's just the kind of a person Who calls us away from our unexamined lives and makes us think uncomfortable thoughts. His refusal to accept the table manners of the religious authorities here in the Gospel of Mark reminds me of this story a woman named Marcy Lay once told me.

Marcy Lay directed the church choir. She is a sage of a person, wise and faithful. After a grueling debate over the color of poinsettias to decorate the sanctuary of our church in Tennessee, white as it had been for years or new and risqué red, she told me about how in her family, at holiday dinners, someone had to cut the last three inches off the ham before cooking it: not on the big side, but on the little side where the bone might stick out. Someone had to go through the trouble of cutting three of four inches off the ham before it could be cooked in her family. That's just what everyone did, it was the family tradition, until somebody – it was probably her sister's boyfriend or some other interloper – asked, "That's silly. Why are you doing that?"

No one had ever asked that question.

You weren't supposed to ask, and so no one was really prepared to give an answer. Fortunately, out of the uncomfortable silence, Grandma piped up: "Years ago, the biggest pan I had was about four inches too short for the ham we bought at Christmas, so I just got into the habit of cutting off that end. I don't know why you're still doing it. That pan you have is plenty big enough to fit the whole thing."

Is that the way with any of the traditions in your house?

Do you feel like you must cook macaroni and cheese a certain way?

Is it necessary to mash the potatoes rather than whip them?

Or is your pre-Thanksgiving meal tradition talking about that awful man Cousin Susie brought home for Christmas who asked all those stupid questions. "Thank goodness he's not been back," we all say.

They asked Him, "Why do your disciples not live according to the tradition of the elders, but eat with defiled hands?" He said to them, "You abandon the commandments of God and hold to human tradition."

Do you know how hard it is to tell the difference?

Do you know how difficult it is to let go of any routine in a world like this one?

By now, you've heard that our kids won't be going back to school. I don't know that I've ever looked forward to the tradition of back-to-school shopping. However, not doing it is breaking my heart. This week, our Cece was looking through masks to wear on her first day. Lily was supposed to start at the Sixth Grade Academy. I don't like how they grow up so fast. I want them to stay little for longer, though this feeling of not being able to watch them go through the milestones of life that they're supposed to go through has me all tied up.

I miss the traditions.

I miss our routines.

I miss how normal life felt.

Surely, Jesus can understand that.

Surely, He's not unsympathetic to whatever suffering we feel, regardless of how minor or how major, only in a time like this one, we must always remember that Jesus doesn't care about human traditions. Instead, He cares about the commandments of God.

He cares not nearly so much about getting things back to normal as moving us towards the Kingdom. Therefore, even in a time such as this one when the last thing I want to think about is changing the semblance of a routine that I've managed to establish, Jesus pushes us to ask the question: Are we abandoning the commandments of God to hold onto human tradition?

Are we still cutting off the ends of our hams even though our pan is big enough for the whole thing?

Are we risking our health and the health of our neighbors for some time-honored rituals, which in this moment just don't make any good sense?

Since the *Marietta Daily Journal* doesn't run on Sundays or Mondays anymore, my wife, Sara, very thoughtfully gave me a Sunday subscription to the *Atlanta Journal-Constitution*. I prefer to read my news rather than watch it on TV, and my Sundays have been disrupted enough already, so I've really missed my Sunday paper. I've been enjoying her gift. Then last Sunday, there was a special note from the editor in the AJC:

The first half of 2020 saw people across metro Atlanta face big challenges and do extraordinary things. Parents figured out how to do their jobs from home and guide their children's education at the same time. Families worried about the health of their loved ones. Everyone made sacrifices, with some being hit harder than others. Through all of this, many did their very best work, every day.

I love this paragraph.

I love it because, for one thing, it's just important to stop and reflect on what's happened over the past weeks and months, what we've done and what we're capable of. I also believe that the AJC has it right: through all of this, many did their very best work, every day. That's true of you. That's true of our church.

Last Sunday, the most amazing thing happened.

You've probably heard about it.

Bill Fogarty turned 93 years old. Normally, there would have been a party. Maybe we would have sung him "Happy Birthday" in here. Surely, we all would have shaken his hand or given him a hug to celebrate the gift from God that he is to this church. None of that could happen, but this did: his wonderful daughter Jean and her daughters sent out a message and organized a drive-by birthday party for him. There were so many cars in this parade that we couldn't all make it through the same traffic light. Once we got to his neighborhood, we had to wait all through the streets, preventing people from pulling out of their driveways and causing a traffic jam. Then, when we finally were all there, we all drove past to shout "happy birthday" out the windows of our cars. Driving by, I thought to myself, "This is what church is all about. This is what it means to be in a family of faith."

It couldn't happen like it did before.

It might not happen the way we remember for a very long time, but remember this: Love is the same. We are still First Presbyterian Church. We are still one holy people who worship God together. We are still changing lives with faith, hope, and love. No virus is ever going to stop that.

In this strange and challenging season, when, as soon as you've given everything you thought you could give, you are asked to sacrifice even more, do not cling so tightly to tradition, ritual, or what we've called normal that you go down with this temporal world that we've always known would fall away. Cling tightly this day, not to human tradition, but to the promises of God.

For everything is changing, but God is the same yesterday, today, and forever.

Amen.

The Joseph Narrative

Whenever I think of the Joseph narrative, which begins with a young son, spoiled by his father, and ends with that same boy, now grown and leading the Egyptian empire, I remember a Walter Brueggemann quote: "The main character in this narrative is not Joseph or even his father, Jacob, but God."

God is the one moving this narrative from the book of Genesis along, just as God is moving our stories along. That was important for me to remember as the pandemic stretched on.

Pushing the Date Back
Romans 8: 26-39 and Genesis 29: 15-28
Preached on July 26, 2020

Last Tuesday was my 40th birthday. Just before, last Sunday morning, I walked outside to find 40 pink flamingoes, a handful of metal pigs, and a cardboard cut-out of my 18-year-old self gracing our front yard. Apparently, three members of our church staff woke up early on Sunday morning to surprise me, marking my 40th birthday the best birthday I've ever had.

It was.

Truly.

From you, I've received so many cards that I haven't been able to open them all. I was serenaded by Jeffrey and Gordon Meeks on the piano and violin, as well as Van Pearlberg on the accordion. I've been so moved by the way you have marked this milestone birthday that I haven't even been sad as I think about how different my 18-year-old body looks from my 40-year-old one.

Sara had me go outside to stand next to my 18-year-old frame.

As I compare my 40-year-old body to my 18-year-old body, it's clear that my 18-year-old stomach is flatter, my 18-year-old arms are more muscular, and my 18-year-old head has much more hair, so looking at the cardboard cutout version of my old self has been cause for important reflection this week.

Not only has it made me want to join a gym and to start using Rogaine, it's also made me wonder, if I could go back to talk with my 18-year-old self, what would I say other than "Enjoy that full head of hair while you have it?"

Maybe I would say that, and, more importantly, I think I would also tell the 18-year-old Joe Evans not to do anything too stupid as he galivants around Marietta, Georgia in front of the members of First Presbyterian Church because in just a few years he's going to come back to become their pastor.

Honestly, I can think of many things I'd do differently, only today, I feel strongly that the best thing to tell my 18-year-old self would be, "Don't be too hard on yourself because everything is teaching you something. Everyone has something to tell you. Keep going and keep learning. Don't avoid challenges and don't have too many regrets because somehow God is at work in all of it."

Do you believe that?

I do.

Or I do most of the time.

Sometimes I fall into the thinking that it would be nice to have a time machine; that it would be wonderful to have a time machine that I might go back in time to tell my old self: "On that Mexico Mission trip, don't let Jenny Pratt take a picture of you in an old cut-up t-shirt, jean shorts, and a cowboy hat. It will come back to haunt you on your 40th birthday in the form of a cardboard cut-out."

That's maybe what we'd like to do. Meanwhile, we're being shaped by all kinds of things and all kinds of people, and just as God's purposes are advanced by the good things that He does, sometimes God takes the bad things and does something good out of them.

The question our Scripture lessons for today ask is: Could God be at work in all of it? Has God used any number of both miracles and tragic events to shape and change us into the people we are today?

My 18-year-old self had not yet met Sara Hernandez, who would become one of my life's greatest miracles, but neither had my 18-year-old self seen planes fly into the Twin Towers. Neither had he learned much about disease or despair. Today, as we look back on our lives, can we be bold to see God at work in the bad people, like Laban, or the tragic events, like being tricked by him, to internalize Paul's conviction from the book of Romans, "that all things work together for good?"

That's a tall order.

That's a great challenge.

Yet in a time of global pandemic, this is the question we must be asking ourselves because if we don't dare to see God at work today, then God's light may shine upon us without us noticing. We may miss out on important opportunities to grow in our faith.

Back to Jacob.

I know he might have told his 18-year-old self to avoid Laban, though his life would have been so different if he had. Thinking about Laban and the story of Jacob and Rachel in our second Scripture lesson, I'm glad that Jacob and Rachel didn't come to me for their pre-marital counseling. Can you imagine? What a mess.

Some of their relationship was typical enough.

It started when he saw her.

Maybe it was love at first sight.

Immediately, he wanted to impress her, so he rolled the stone away from the mouth of the well and watered her sheep for her. It's the perfect beginning of a romance, and those of you who know what it is to fall in love can think back to what he did that first got your attention, or how when you saw her, you would have lifted any number of stones to get her to look your way. Jacob and Rachel have their first kiss that very day. In Genesis chapter 29, Jacob kissed Rachel. Scripture tells us that when it happened, Jacob "wept aloud."

It was as every first kiss should be.

Then, before things go any further, Jacob goes to meet her father. Rachel's father agrees to allow this relative stranger to marry his daughter when Jacob offers to work seven years in exchange for her hand in marriage. This is the part of the story where I can imagine Jacob wanting a time machine. He says, "I will serve you seven years for your younger daughter Rachel." Then Laban said, "It is better that I should give her to you than that I should give her to any other man; stay with me." Never mind that these two men are talking about this poor young woman like she's a piece of property or an old Ford truck, a deal is struck. An agreement is made. Jacob is ready to do what he needs to do so he goes and does it, only we know it won't be that easy because it almost never is. In fact, these seven years make me think of what we were all told at the beginning of the COVID-19 outbreak: "Just stay at home for three or four weeks and this thing will be over."

Do you remember them telling us that?

Then three or four weeks stretched out into three and four months. Now we're being told we're still not getting anywhere. Likewise, at the end of seven years Jacob goes to Laban to make good on their agreement and Laban gives him Leah.

There's always something that makes a marriage hard.

There's always something that must be overcome.

Still, never in premarital counseling have I heard a couple say: "Pastor, the thing that makes our relationship complicated is that he's already married to my sister." Can you imagine? Had I been doing their premarital counseling, I'd ask for clarification: "So, Jacob, you were tricked into marrying her sister by your father-in-law?" "And you didn't realize it wasn't Rachel until the morning after your wedding night?" "And you're still married to Leah?"

What are we to say about these things?

Surely, we expect better of the heroes of the Bible.

Surely, we expect better out of our family members.

Surely, we expect more out of life; however, it only gets worse, more twisted, more complicated, for at times, God's people, regardless of the generation, all wonder to themselves, "God, why are you doing this to me?"

No doubt, like Jacob, if we had a time machine and could go back to tell our 18-year-old selves something, some of us would go back to voice a warning: "I know she caught your eye, but keep walking." "I know he seems nice enough, but don't trust him." "I know it's dark in the tent, but before you do anything, make sure she's not your sister-in-law."

Likewise, there are plenty of things I would love to do over again, and there are some people I would love to have avoided, though sometimes, in dealing with difficult issues, we're actually dealing with ourselves.

It's true.

It's true that Laban tricked Jacob, but whom did Jacob trick?

As we read the book of Genesis and consider Jacob's character, we remember that before he met Rachel, he had already stolen his older brother's inheritance. Therefore, I believe we must wonder if it might be that what Jacob hates most about Laban and his tricks is what Jacob hates most within himself. What he learns then in being tricked by Laban is how he must have made his brother feel. What he learns in getting hurt is what hurt feels like. What he learns in having to put his life on hold is that life requires that we not just get by but grow.

Today, what I realize about this time of quarantine, is that as much as I want it to be over, and as much as I wish it would have never happened; that as much as I might wish that someone could go back in time to stop that virus from ever spreading, what we Christians must be bold to do is to consider that in this moment, it's as though God has hit the reset button on this nation.

That in this moment, it's as though God has hit the reset button on our lives.

Before now, few among us had time for self-reflection.

Few among us had the chance to consider not only where we've been but where we're going. In this moment, when it seems most of us have plenty of time, turn off the TV and put down your phone for just a moment to ask yourself: "What is God trying to teach me today?"

In looking at that cardboard cutout of my 18-year-old self, I see that despite whatever mistakes I had made or was yet to make because of that Mexico

Mission Trip I was on when the picture was taken, I was already learning that the way toward a full and abundant life was marked, not by selfishness, but service; that the way toward happiness is a movement away from self and towards the other; that life is not to be lived by tricking people as Jacob tricked Esau or as Laban tricked Jacob, but in loving my neighbor as myself, regardless of who my neighbor is.

In this self-centered, defensive, ego-driven culture of ours, God is giving us a chance to choose a new path.

Don't spend so much time wishing you could go back to change what has already happened that you forfeit your chance to start making a better future today. And know that as you grow and change, as you learn and live, God is with you fulfilling His promises.

Halleluiah.

Amen.

The Dreamer Had It Right
Romans 10: 5-15 and Genesis 37: 1-5 and 12-28
Preached on August 9, 2020

There's an expression I remember from Tennessee that reminds me of Joseph. Based on what we've just read, he seems to have possessed that mix of ignorance or arrogance which rightfully earned him the spite of his brothers and would have inspired the use of that Tennessee expression: "Don't ever be a small-town guy with a big city haircut."

Have you ever heard someone say that?

It may be that no one uses that expression outside of Middle-Tennessee, but we all should because it's important to warn people that not everything that comes with a fancy haircut, a nice new car, or a special robe, is good. We need more ways to express the sentiment that if you have champagne tastes but brothers who only drink Pabst Blue Ribbon beer, they're likely to make fun of you. It's important to warn people like Joseph that while any one of us may have a dream of being bigger and better than our families, we must be careful about how we tell them all about it. Best case scenario, this Joseph from a small town with a big-city, long-sleeved, extra-special robe will inspire the people who love him to kindly, patronizingly smile while he tells them his grandiose dreams. However, our second Scripture lesson warns that in the worst-case scenario, they may try to kill him.

I don't know exactly why human society holds back the dreamers this way. Is it because the dreamers make the rest feel small? Whatever it is about them or us, I know that it was merciful that his brothers only threw Joseph down into an empty pit until a band of traveling Ishmaelite salesmen wandered by. That doesn't sound merciful, selling someone into slavery, but they were planning to kill him because no one likes a small-town guy with a big city haircut, and everyone resents the youngest child who announces: "One day, you'll all be bowing down before me."

You can't say that.

You just can't.

So I don't really feel sorry for Joseph.

You could make the argument that I should, but I don't. However, certainly, his father did. Reading this second Scripture lesson from his perspective or from the brother's perspective tells two different versions of the same story, and there are a few ways to read this passage of Scripture from the book of Genesis. On reading this first chapter of the beautiful rollercoaster ride that is Joseph's story in the book of Genesis, we're likely to either resonate with him, the young, long-sleeved, dreamer; his jealous brothers; or his elderly, doting father, who couldn't help but spoil the child of his old age a little bit. I truly and easily understand where the brothers are coming from; however, to get to the fullness of this Scripture lesson, we must also consider the perspective of Jacob, Joseph's father.

At this point in the book of Genesis, he's called Israel, for from his sons will come the 12 tribes of this chosen nation. When those brothers rise up against one of their own, they show their father, Jacob or Israel, Joseph's cloak dipped in goat's blood. Notice, though, they don't have to explain anything. Did you pick up on that? Jacob, as he is called earlier, or Israel, as he is renamed by God, reaches his own conclusions about his young son's fate based on the evidence at hand. He takes one look at a bloody cloak and quickly considers it in light of the harsh realities of the merciless world he lived in.

Maybe you can understand how his mind was working.

Bloody cloak plus rumors of a wild beast that lurked around the outskirts of the land of Canaan equals the conclusion that his son has been eaten. Just as COVID-19 plus protests, unemployment plus quarantine, or homeschooling plus a failed wireless connection can have any one of us feeling like the world is ending.

Has it ever been the case with you that you took in the information at hand and reached a logical conclusion, only to find out later that it was exactly the wrong one?

That's the story of Jacob really because Joseph wasn't dead.

Before we get to that, fully consider what was going on in his father's mind that made it so easy for him to believe that he was. Jacob knew the world to be a harsh place. We think back on the stories we already know about him, and it makes sense that a man willing to trick his own brother and manipulate his own father, who was himself fooled by his father-in-law and then wrestled with God by the bank of a river, would surely come to the conclusion that the world doesn't liberally hand out blessings. No, if you want something, you had better get it, and if you quit fighting, you should expect the worst.

Turn your back on this world and expect to be stabbed. That was Jacob's philosophy, and while he had begun to believe in forgiveness when his brother Esau chose mercy, just after that his daughter Dinah was abused, and then his father died.

Life taught him that two plus two is four, and bloody cloak of favorite son equals tragedy.

Surely, some would call that way of thinking logic or knowledge based in experience. Whatever it was, and no matter how much sense it made, Jacob was wrong because Joseph wasn't dead, so on the one hand, we have Jacob's logic, but on the other hand, we have Joseph's dream.

You know what's wonderful about dreams?

Sometimes dreams look at the exact same evidence and come back with an exactly opposite conclusion. Joseph, despite his brothers, never stopped dreaming. As the Ishmaelite caravan carried him to some unknown place, he never gave up hope. Then, as he was sold to Potiphar, wrongly accused by Potiphar's wife, and then dragged off to prison, did this young man give up on his future? Did he give up on the dream?

I feel like I do all the time.

There are plenty of images in Scripture that make me profoundly hopeful, but that I give up on as soon as the tide turns against me. Christ speaks of loving your neighbor as yourself, then I receive the wrong email at the wrong moment, and it seems nearly impossible. Likewise, I read about the coming Kingdom, how our God is bringing fullness and restoration to each corner of creation; though I then think about virtual learning and see a future of zombie kids addicted to computer screens, or I think about in-person learning, and all I can see are outbreaks of a virus we can't seem to get a hold of.

There's a fair amount of Jacob in me, for some days I look at the evidence at hand, and I assume the worst, but Jacob was wrong, you see.

Jacob was wrong, and I must be willing to consider that I might be wrong, too.

It has happened before.

Once, I got home from church, and standing in the driveway, I bent over to pick up something from the ground and split my pants. There are at least two ways to explain something like that: Either the suit was cheap, or the guy wearing it, me, had expanded. As it turns out in this case, both parties were guilty as charged, but I hope you're getting my point.

Sometimes we make assumptions, and sometimes our assumptions are wrong, so acknowledge this with me: the way we view the world we live in colors the way we understand the information we receive.

What we already believe changes the way we see the future.

And the truth, while Scripture says it will set us free, also demands that we rethink all kinds of things. Sometimes the truthdemands that we change the way we see the whole world.

Thinking of the truth, can you imagine if back in February someone had said that your kids won't be going back to school in their classrooms next year?

Many of you will start working from home.

You might get together with people, but you won't want to shake their hands, and facemasks are going to become commonplace in grocery stores.

Can you imagine if someone from the future visited us five months ago to report that everyone you know, even your grandmother, is going to learn how to use a program on their computer called *Zoom*?

You know that list of projects around your house? You're going to do all of them out of sheer boredom.

By the way, *Netflix* doesn't have enough content to provide for what's about to happen.

Lies are sometimes easier to believe than the truth, especially if there's enough evidence pushing your assumptions, especially if there are enough dots to connect, especially if all you have to do just accept what's right in front of you rather than lift up your eyes to the heavens. That's maybe the difference between Jacob and his young son Joseph in this passage from Genesis. Jacob is willing and ready to believe the worst from what's right in front of him while Joseph refuses to give up on a dream despite what's right in front of him.

Do you know anyone like that?

Sure, you do.

She's maybe five years old, and she would be going off to start Kindergarten ifshe could. Regardless, she's still off to conquer the world. Ask her what she wants to be when she grows up, and she'll tell you, "I want to be a doctor and a nurse and a teacher and a babysitter." If you could ask a whole group of them, "Who here plays a musical instrument?" every one of them would raise his hand.

Who here has a friend in his class?

Who feels loved by her teacher?

Who here knows that tomorrow will be even better than today?

School didn't start this year like it always does, and I feel sure that means the children of this church will miss out on some of the lessons they should be learning. Regardless, let me make this suggestion: Today, we need to be learning a lesson from them because too often, we grownups look at the data at hand and see the worst. Too often, we cling to logic rather than hope. Too many of us base our projections on numbers and not faith, so consider for just a moment a child who will look into a mud puddle and see the perfect filling or a pie or who will see a prolonged time of quarantine as a good reason to spend more time with her family.

I don't know what you're using to understand the world out there today with all its horror and all its tragedy, but let me tell you this: these days, a five-year-old may have an edge, for if nothing else, this Scripture lesson from the book of Genesis tells us that the dreamer had it right.

Amen.

They Didn't Get What They Deserved
Romans 11: 1-2a, 29-32 and Genesis 45: 1-15
Preached on August 16, 2020

I want to begin this sermon by telling you about a young woman, a friend of a friend, who had just moved to New York City. She was living in her very first apartment, which was just large enough to sleep in, working her very first job that paid her just enough to get by. You might remember what that was like, so you'll understand why, when her boss asked her to stay in her apartment for a couple weeks to care for her cat while she went on vacation, this young woman jumped at the chance.

The apartment was wonderful. Unlike hers, it was air-conditioned. It had, not just a microwave, but a full kitchen. There was no roommate. Plus, it had wireless internet that actually worked and a great, big TV. Such luxury, and all she had to do was keep the cat. The only problem was that on the second or third day, the cat died.

She felt horrible, as you can imagine, and rehearsed the phone call a few dozen times before finally calling her boss, the cat's owner, to deliver the bad news. Fortunately for the young woman, her boss understood completely as the cat was 16 years old. Her boss' only request was that she go ahead and deliver the cat's body to the vet's office where they would handle the remains. Relieved to be done with such a sensitive phone call, she hung up before thinking through one big, important detail. The vet was across town, and she didn't have a car.

How would she transport the cat there?

She couldn't walk because it was too far.

She didn't have enough money for a taxi, and even if she did, she couldn't just hold a dead cat in her arms, so she looked around the apartment and finally found an old briefcase. She put the cat in it and went down to the subway, got on the train and sat down. The briefcase was on the floor between her feet, and she tried hard not to act like anything at all was the matter.

As the train rolled along, a nice-looking young man sat down next to her. After a little while, he nudged her and looking down at the briefcase, asked her if she was on her way to work. "Yes, I am, as a matter of fact," she replied with a little too much confidence, "just going into the office with my trusty laptop," she said looking down at the briefcase. Then she asked what he was on the way to. He was headed to the Metropolitan Museum of Art to enjoy the Egypt exhibit since it was his day off, or something like that. Well, she loved the Met, too, and it turned out that's not the only thing that they had in common, so at some point in the conversation, this young woman began to wonder if she was about to be asked out on her first date in New York City with a dead cat between her feet. However, before that could happen, the train came to a stop, the young man snatched that briefcase and ran off the train, never to be seen again.

Now I tell you this story because it's not every day that the thief gets what he deserves.

It's not in every story that justice, precious justice, is served, so I tell you this story today because we have been wronged. A faceless enemy assails us. More than 160,000 Americans are dead, parents are trying to work, kids are home from school, and I've thought of worse things that I wish would happen to some of the people responsible than opening up a briefcase to find a dead cat.

That's why I love the story I just told you.

I've told it so many times that Sara never wants to hear it again, though I keep telling it because I love it when the bad guy doesn't get away.

Can you imagine what Joseph was hoping would happen to his brothers? As you know well, his story begins when he was the little brother who didn't know when to stop talking about himself, so his brothers helped him find his way into a pit with no water in it. You can imagine how he looked up from the bottom waiting for the joke to be over and saw his brothers looking down on him, glad to have put him in his place. It turns out they weren't just joking. They meant to get rid of him, so there were chains next as they sold him for silver coins, then a long journey to a world he'd never seen, surrounded by words he couldn't understand, and he was helpless to do anything about it. He went from the chains of a slave to the cell of a prisoner wrongly accused, though neither the rats nor the guards cared that he was innocent.

Each day passed slowly.

Each day, he was hungry.

Each day, he was alone with only the memories of the brothers who got him there in the first place and the thought of what he would do to them if he ever had the chance. You can imagine that he was ready for the moment when he would finally see them again. He probably had rehearsed his words and actions through a million times before.

You know what vengeance is like.

Do you remember from *The Princess Bride*, "Hello, my name is Inigo Montoya. You killed my father. Prepare to die."? How many times had Joseph thought it through? How many times had he rehearsed the words? How sweet was the thought of his revenge? Yet, from his seat of power, having risen through the ranks of the Egyptian hierarchy, he not only has the faces of his brothers looking down on him from the edge of that pit in his mind's eye, he sees also the hand of God leading him, sustaining and preserving him, lifting him up for just such a time as this.

With his brothers before him and at his mercy, he threw out his prepared speech for something else: "I am your brother, Joseph, whom you sold into Egypt. And now do not be distressed, or angry with yourselves, because you sold me here; for God sent me before you to preserve life… God sent me before you to preserve for you a remnant on earth, and to keep alive many survivors. So it was not you who sent me here, but God."

If our daughter Lily had been there, she would have said, "Wait, what?"

Such perspective.

Such maturity.

Such faith.

Truly, his example is a timely one for us today because I know what some people would like to do to our school superintendents. I know what others would like to do to the governor. I know how some of you all feel about people who don't wear face masks in the grocery store. Now is a time when we find ourselves at the bottom of a pit. Without a clear way out, what is there to do but locate a target for our frustration and plot our revenge? I can think of plenty of people who I hope open their briefcases tomorrow to find dead cats, though blame won't get us as far as mercy because blame points a finger at the failure of humans, while mercy opens our eyes to the power of God.

And God is at work among us.

The story I told about the cat and the briefcase, the first time I remember telling it was at Buck and Cindy Buchanan's house just before they moved to California. That was 15 or 16 years ago. That I've been telling the same story for 15 or 16 years is one thing; another is that after 15 or 16 years, they're back here in Marietta, and so am I.

I don't know who you are blaming for this nightmare we're stuck in, but I urge you to think like Joseph today and the way the hand of God is moving all of us according to his purpose.

Stop blaming.

Stop plotting revenge.

Stop harping on human power, for God is at work, and in this moment of true powerlessness, when we cannot climb our way out, we can still choose to be faithful.

I just learned this morning that when John Lewis walked across the Edmund Pettus Bridge, he expected to spend the night in jail, so he carried with him two books: one was political, the other was *The Seven Story Mountain* by a monk named Thomas Merton. In that book, Merton wrote, "People have no idea what one saint can do: for sanctity is stronger than the whole of hell."

My friends, we are standing at the edge of it, and it may seem as though we are powerless to do much about it, but we are not without a choice in what we do. Choose today to be more holy, more merciful, more kind, and more faithful. When you watch the world and those who scurry across your TV screen, don't look for humans to disappoint you because they always will. Instead, look for the hand at work in all of this, for He never will disappoint you, nor does He slumber, nor does He sleep.

Someday, we'll hear about how all this could have been avoided, and we'll have the chance to point our fingers at those who are to blame, but until we know how to forgive, we'll never deserve the grace that's been provided. Joseph's brothers deserved punishment, but they did not get what they deserved.

Neither have we.

We have been forgiven, and we must learn to forgive.

We have been redeemed, and we must trust God to redeem us again. For Joseph was led by the hand of God to save His people, and by the hand of God, we will be saved, so choose faith this day. Choose faith.

Amen.

Moses

Looking back on these sermons today, I see how appropriate it was to focus on the books of Exodus and Deuteronomy at the time they were preached. Exodus describes the Hebrew peoples' journey from slavery in Egypt to freedom in the Promised Land. As I preached these sermons, the Session (the governing body of a Presbyterian Church) of First Presbyterian Church was making decisions to help the congregation return to worship in-person after having worshiped only at home for almost six months. This return was phased. At first, there was no singing, no bulletins or offering plates, the numbers were capped, masks were required, and the seating was assigned. For the first, time members were making reservations to come to church. It was all strange and many were scared, but what I will always remember is how hard this congregation was willing to fight to worship their God.

Say Her Name

Romans 12: 1-8 and Exodus 1: 8 – 2: 10

Preached on August 23, 2020

This second Scripture lesson I've just read begins a series of sermons based on the book of Exodus. In this well-known account, which begins in the first chapter, we remember that from the time Joseph saved his brothers and their families from famine, Jacob and his descendants lived in Egypt. They prospered there, probably without thinking too much about what would have been their homeland, the land promised by God to Abraham that was said to be flowing with milk and honey. In Egypt, Hebrew children were born with no memory of any land besides the fields and riverbanks nourished by the Nile River. There, grandchildren forgot the stories of Jacob and Esau to learn stories about Ra and Ramses the Great.

Like the immigrants of any time or place, they likely felt the pressure to lose their accents and just fit in. You can imagine that Joseph's young descendants didn't want to invite their Egyptian school friends over for dinner, afraid that grandma would cook some strange food from a far-away place. Life as newcomers to a foreign land is like that. Among the Hebrew people who settled in Goshen, you can hear grandparents interrupt their grandchildren's conversations concerning the fastest chariots or the best places to swim in the Nile with old stories about a homeland and a promise from God. Maybe the grandparents wanted them to remember and to prepare themselves to go back one day, but the grandchildren just wanted to fit in because that's what grandchildren want to do.

However, if a cat crawls into an oven to deliver her litter, they're still kittens, not muffins. In the same way, just being born in Egypt doesn't make one Egyptian any more than being born at our local Kennestone Hospital makes you one of the Old Marietta crowd. In fact, just as the Israelites lived in Egypt, you can live somewhere for years and never quite belong, though we all want to belong. Whether in the place we were born or in the place we've adopted, we all want to fit in, so while my father-in-law, who moved from Columbia, South America to Knoxville, was always planning on moving back home eventually, he did try to fit in as a college student at the University of Tennessee, but it was hard.

He landed in Knoxville to study architecture while still learning the English language. Not yet grasping all the nuances, a couple of nice church ladies asked him on the sidewalk if he'd been "saved." He assumed they were asking about his bank account. Likewise, one of his first times through the cafeteria line at breakfast, he asked for a biscuit with "groovy" instead of a biscuit with gravy. This was the 60s, so you can imagine how he'd make the mistake. Fortunately, the cafeteria lady on the other side of the serving line laughed, and so did he because he's the kind of guy who can laugh at himself. Even still, fitting in is a serious business.

Nobody wants to feel like the new guy forever. No one wants to go into the Marietta Fruit Company or any other local restaurant without getting served. No one likes to be the person who never really fits in and always stands out. We all are trying to be a part of the group because that's just what human beings want to do. Sooner or later, we all want to be one of *them*. For that reason and many others these, midwives are worth remembering.

Say their names with me: Shiphrah and Puah.

I know you're Presbyterians who aren't used to talking during the sermon, so just whisper them with me, "Shiphrah and Puah."

It's important that we know their names and that we remember them. After all, besides Moses, their names are the only names listed in this second Scripture lesson. Moses is named, but his father isn't. His mother is mentioned, but she isn't named. His sister and Pharaoh's daughter are both referred to but remain nameless. Notice that not even Pharaoh is named in our second Scripture lesson. He's just Pharaoh. Which one? To the Bible, it doesn't matter because he doesn't matter, or not nearly as much as these two midwives matter.

Shiphrah and Puah.

Say their names.

Remember their names because they had this chance to please the king of Egypt, but they chose instead to honor their God.

Can you imagine what that must have felt like?

Can you imagine how terrifying it must have been?

Do you have some idea of what pleasing him could have meant?

Surely, they were tempted.

As the outsiders, surely, they imagined that pleasing Pharaoh could have been one small step towards acceptance into the mainstream. To these two midwives, being on his radar was momentous enough. Then they were summoned by him. That they had the chance to do something for him would have been viewed as an opportunity to capitalize on by any with thoughts of social advancement. Regardless of their aspirations, certainly they feared displeasing him. Already, he had proved himself merciless by ordering the execution of babies. Either way, the pressure to do as he commanded must have been profound. Yet, to gain some sense of what they were surely feeling, we need only think about the social pressure our foremothers must have felt.

Last week, the paper published some reflections on 100 years of women's suffrage in Georgia. The paper published some of their names: Mary Latimer McClendon, Mary McCurdy, Helen Augusta Howard, Adella Hunt Logan, Lucy Craft Laney, and Janie Porter Barrett. Their names are unfamiliar because we haven't been saying them enough. However, in 1974, former President Jimmy Carter, Georgia governor at the time, selected a portrait of one of them, Lucy Craft Laney, to be displayed in the Georgia State Capitol along with the Rev. Henry McNeal Turner and the Rev. Martin Luther King. They were the first African Americans to have their portraits hung in the building, but remember especially her name. She founded Atlanta's first school for Black children, as well as the first kindergarten and the first nursing training programs for Black women in Augusta. She was a leader within the National Association for Colored Women, and she helped get women everywhere the vote.

What strikes me about her and all the others like her is what they risked advancing a cause they believed in.

What inspires me is how they looked towards the future with hope and were willing to sacrifice to get there.

What defies my ambivalence and pushes me past indifference is how, though surely some rendered them powerless, they were powerful, and while surely their husbands, fathers, and brothers wanted them to keep quiet, they would not be silenced.

Another suffragette, Helen Augusta Howard, was sentenced to a year in prison. Her brothers claimed that she was mentally unsound. Why? It's because some would call a woman willing to defy any pharaoh completely insane, but do you know how Scripture renders such women?

As faithful.

As worthy of our admiration.

Say their names.

For just as a part of them must have been ready to do what Pharoah asked, there's a part of all of us ready to walk down the easy path towards acceptance of what is and away from who we are and who we were created to be. Just as a part of them must have wanted to just go with the flow, they could see beyond the world as it was and knew they must not settle in, for they were on their way to the Promised Land.

Peer pressure in high school is so hard because while you're in high school, it feels like those four years are all that matters. Not being accepted feels like the end of the world, only we all must learn to deal with such pressure because it never really goes away.

At work is the pressure to please the boss.

Around the neighborhood pool is the pressure to look like everyone else.

Then when talking politics, we're never just talking about whom we're voting for, we're talking about whether, based on whom we've picked, we'll be invited back over for dinner again.

Despite whatever Pharaoh threatened or promised, they chose to remain Shiphrah and Puah.

Say their names.

Remember their names and be like them; let the God Who created you define who you are, not the world that surrounds you. They made the choice to save those Hebrew babies. They chose to listen to their hearts rather than the voice of a sin-sick world, and that same choice is ours today. The Apostle Paul said it this way: "Do not be conformed to this world, but be transformed by the renewing of your minds, so that you may discern what is the will of God – what is good and acceptable and perfect." Do not be conformed to this world, for you don't belong to this world any more than Moses belonged to the Pharaoh's palace.

Can't you imagine him there?

He knew what he had to do to maintain his place in those privileged halls, but how could he when Shiphrah and Puah had sacrificed their lives for him? How could any of us just sit back in indifference to the evil around us when so many mothers, daughters, and sisters sacrificed themselves to get us where we are today. Think for just a moment about them.

Who loved you into existence?

Who was she?

What did she do?

What did she sacrifice for you?

Say her name.

Then, live in such a way that you might deserve the sacrifice she made.

Ours is a culture where it's hard to speak out for the humanity of all people because Pharoah is pulling us towards silent conformity. Yet, how would our mother feel if despite all her labor we stopped working for justice? In our culture of conformity, do not be conformed to this world, but honor the God Who created you, the One Who gave His very life that you would be saved just as Moses was.

Say their names:

Siphrah and Puah.

Mary Latimer McClendon, Mary McCurdy, Helen Augusta Howard, Adella Hunt Logan, Lucy Craft Laney, Janie Porter Barrett, Breonna Taylor, and so many others. Say their names, and may justice rain down on all God's precious children.

Amen.

Who Am I That I Should Go?
Romans 12: 9-21 and Exodus 3: 1-15
Preached on August 30, 2020

Lately I've really been wanting to take a trip to the beach so I can dig a hole in the sand and stick my head in it. Not for long; just for a couple hours. Maybe one afternoon with my head in the sand because I'm ready for a break from all of it.

Now, on top of a viral pandemic, for some people there's a hurricane.

On top of having kids home from school, last Monday morning there was a big *Zoom* outage. Not only are we stuck at home, but it rained all day Tuesday, so we were even more confined to the house than usual.

Our hospital is still full, and according to the *Marietta Daily Journal*, in desperation, some COVID-19 sufferers are resorting to drinking bleach.

Plus, this past week another black man was shot by police officers, only our national conversation concerning race doesn't seem to be going anywhere because we can't agree on enough to form anything more than an argument, so I'd just like to go stick my head in the sand at the beach.

I'd like to escape everything for just a minute.

Concerning the headlines of the past week, certainly I'm thankful that our own Keli Gambrill, County Commissioner, came up with a plan to distribute $4.8 million dollars in grants to struggling homeowners, but before I get too hopeful about such a loving response and such courageous leadership in a leadership vacuum, first I'd just like a little bit of time to put my head in the sand.

Do you know what I mean?

Moses did.

Moses must have known exactly what I'm feeling, which might be how you're feeling right now. He found himself in a complex situation he didn't know how to deal with, and so he just ran off to watch a flock of sheep for a while. The Bible says: "Moses was keeping the flock of his father-in-law Jethro, the priest of Midian; [and] he led his flock beyond the wilderness." What that means is that he had made it to the beach, but not just to the beach, beyond the beach. It means he didn't just go on a vacation but built for himself a great big hole in the sand that he could live down in forever.

It's not a bad idea.

He left, and that worked just fine for Moses until one of his sheep ran off and he stumbled upon a bush that burned a bright flame without being consumed.

Can you imagine it?

Curiosity can be dangerous this way: It might lead you out of your hole in the sand and to a place where you could get hurt. That's why you must be careful about curiosity.

Once, my mother- and father-in-law brought a new puppy home, and she was curious, poking her nose around rocks and into holes on the ground. Before long, a snake bit her right on the nose. Along those same lines, I remember a drive through the Whitlock Heights neighborhood. Several cars were stopped, and a group of people were standing around looking at something in the middle of the street. Naturally, I got out of my car to see what all the excitement was about, and next thing I knew, I was elected to try and remove an alligator snapping turtle from the middle of the road. It came out of the creek nearby the street where the Callaways and the Tuckers live. I hope they lock their doors at night because that thing was a monster.

But back to the point: curiosity is a dangerous thing.

You go looking around corners, get out of your car to see what everyone else is so interested in, or just go sniffing around some new place, and anything can happen. The same kind of thing can happen at a church. A curious person sticks her nose in the door of a church, and who knows what might happen next?

This is a true story.

The Rev. Sarah Hayden, a seminary classmate of mine, once told the story of how her family came to join their First Presbyterian Church. A new church building had been under construction near their neighborhood, and when the construction was finished and the opening worship service was scheduled, her father suggested that they go and check it out. The family walked in and approached a man holding a stack of bulletins by the door into the sanctuary, but instead of handing each member of the family a bulletin, this man handed Sarah's father the whole stack saying, "You must be the one who's supposed to hand out the bulletins."

"Actually, no, I'm not," her father said, "We've never been here before, and we just wanted to check it out."

"Well," the man said, "you hand out the bulletins," and so he did.

That was years ago. Her family found a home there. Sarah's now a Presbyterian minister, and I think her family are still members of that very church. That's how curiosity is.

You see something interesting and decide to see what it's all about, and next thing you know, your life goes in a direction you never could have expected.

Maybe you find your way home.

That's how it was for Moses.

He was as far away from Pharaoh as he could get. Not just in the wilderness, but beyond the wilderness. He wanted not to think about the Israelite family of his birth nor the family who adopted him. He couldn't stand the thought of that day when his worlds collided: his Hebrew birth family and his Egyptian adopted family. He wanted to escape the day when he lost his temper and killed the Egyptian who was beating a Hebrew slave. He tried to leave all that behind just as he left behind the body of that Egyptian taskmaster, hiding his corpse in the sand.

There he was.

He was beyond the wilderness trying to forget or escape, but curiosity brought him right back to the place he didn't want to remember.

At the sight of the burning bush, Moses said, "I must turn aside and look at this great sight, and see why the bush is not burned up," but this curiosity, like all curiosity has the potential to be, led Moses into the presence of God. Once we find ourselves in the presence of God, it's best to be prepared for life to move in directions we never could have expected.

That how it was with me.

We just went to this church when I was kid. It was nice. On the way here on Sunday mornings, I'd read the funny papers in the back seat of our minivan. When we got here, I'd sometimes have donuts and would sing in Sunday school. In the service, we'd stand up and turn to the right hymns in the hymnals. I'd bow my head and close my eyes when I was supposed to, and I knew the service was almost over when Dr. Jim Speed stood in front of us with his arms up saying words not so different from our first Scripture lesson as his benediction: "Hold fast to that which is true. Render to no one evil for evil," he'd say, and he'd say it as though we were actually supposed to do it. Go poking your nose in a hole, and you might get bit by a snake.

Walk over to a group of people looking at something in the street and end up responsible for a snapping turtle.

Get out of bed, turn on your computer, and join a church service.

Actually listen to the words of the benediction and learn what it means to be a Christian.

After being a part of this virtual service, it's possible to go on with your day no differently from how you were when you woke up this morning, but if you're open to hearing God's voice, you'd better be careful, or you'll wind up going places and saying things that will dredge up the past and rechart your future.

That's how it was with me, and that's how it was with Moses.

Moses just wanted a closer look, and next thing he knew, the God of his ancestors was telling him, "The cry of the Israelites has come to me; I have also seen how the Egyptians oppress them. So come, I will send you to Pharaoh to bring my people, the Israelites, out of Egypt." The Lord had heard their cry, and I am confident that the Lord hears the cry of the oppressed today.

The Lord hears the unspoken worries of mothers who are depending on free food distributions so they can save their money and stave off eviction.

The Lord listens to the prayers of the sick who long for a vaccine and turns toward the school child who wants to go back to class but never will, unless the grownups get their act together and stop spreading the virus all over the place.

He bears the quiet weeping of the ones who mourn but can't have a funeral and knows the frustration of those who want a world without racism but lack a clear path to move toward it.

The Lord knows the struggle of the would-be voter who isn't sure whether her vote will even be counted.

We all want to know when is someone going to do something about all of it, when is it going to get better, and where is the one who is going to get us out of this? In a time like this one, it's easy to wonder where God is or if God knows.

Where has God been?

I think I know.

God's been calling, waiting on you and me to get our head out of the sand to answer.

We are all living in this terrifying time. However, we don't need to hide from it. Even if it's just to have a conversation we've been putting off, we must be bold to believe that God will go with us to do the impossible.

Last Sunday, I was invited to join with the members of our church who make up our northern campus. The Big Canoe Neighborhood Group have started calling themselves "FPC North." They invited me up for a cocktail in the driveway, and there we were talking about how hard it is to simply have a conversation. One member of the group has adopted a great phrase for use in these divisive times, "Well, I couldn't disagree more, but we can still be friends." How hard it is to make such bold statements. How much easier it is to stick our heads in the sand, yet my friends, the Lord is doing a new thing, and if we are to be a part of it, we must find a way not to run away from the uncomfortable conversations nor keep our true opinions to ourselves.

Be curious enough to ask yourself: What might God do through us if we're brave enough to answer the call?

What might God do through us if we're bold enough to stand and say what we believe?

What might God do through us if we're just curious enough to follow where He leads?

Amen.

History Repeats Itself, As Does Deliverance
Romans 13: 8-14 and Exodus 12: 1-14
Preached on September 6, 2020

When I got dressed last Monday morning, I put on my funeral suit. I didn't have a funeral to go to, but the occasion warranted my funeral suit. Maybe you heard that someone or some small group of people spray painted swastikas on fences and on the sides of buildings nearby an East Cobb synagogue. As this synagogue, Temple Kol Emeth, is one of the religious groups we partner with to build homes through Habitat for Humanity, I was invited to join a group of politicians, police officers, preachers, rabbis, Imams, and journalists there. We all assembled to show our support to the temple and her congregation and to openly stand against those signs of hatred that remind us of what human beings are capable of when we fail to love our neighbors as ourselves.

It just happens too often, doesn't it?

If you Google the word *genocide*, a list comes up. This list includes Hindus, Muslims, Hutus, Tutsis, Irish, Palestinians, Bosnians, Croats, Tamils, Tartars, and a long list of indigenous people who were murdered with abandon.

Certainly, the genocide of the Jews by the Nazis is the most notorious.

They're by no means alone, but they're the group we think of when remembering hatred and evil. The sign of the swastika reminds all of us of that nightmare when especially Jews, but also gypsies, homosexuals, Poles, and anyone else who was considered less than human was herded up into concentrations camps to be exterminated. Today, most of us see the swastika and remember what should never happen again, though it has, and could, so I put on my funeral suit and drove over to the synagogue.

Everybody was there.

We assembled in the part of the temple we Presbyterians would call the narthex. I walked in with an Imam. We were both running a little late. We made it inside just as it started raining. He had been asked to speak, and I hadn't, though (this is what I want to emphasize) either one of us could have because we people of faith have been trained to respond to those moments in human life that defy easy explanation.

We have been given the words to say to people when there are no words.

We know what to do when it seems like there's nothing that anyone can do.

We religious people testify to a hope that defies explanation.

The way Tom Long, famous preacher and scholar who until recently taught at Emory's Candler School of Theology, described it in his great book about the funeral is that at the grave, there are generally two preachers. One is death, and his sermon is always the same. From the depths of the tomb he says, "This is the end. It's all over. There is no more to say." However, at the grave, there often stands another preacher who reminds those assembled of the One Who rose again. He or she points to the light that shines in the darkness. The ancient words we say are those of a love that can never be conquered, an everlasting life that has no end, and a great company of saints who join the living and the dead in singing a bold Halleluiah.

Our funeral liturgy is no different than our second Scripture lesson; it's a list of instructions for what to say and what to do so that we remember that while history repeats itself, so does deliverance:

Every household in the assembled congregation of Israel shall take part.

They shall have a lamb of their own unless they are too small a family and need to share with their neighbors.

Divide it in proportion to the number of people who shall eat of it.

The lamb should be without blemish, a year-old male from the sheep or from the goats.

Keep it until the fourteenth day of the month.

Slaughter it at twilight.

"This day shall be a day of remembrance for you. You shall celebrate it as a festival to the Lord throughout your generations." Why? It's so that every year, you remember again that just when you start to think that the light is about to go out, God may choose to show up once again.

Don't forget that.

Don't forget something so important in a time like this one.

Still, it's easy to forget, so despite what I know, I walked into that synagogue last Monday morning wondering what anyone could say.

What do you say when hatred rears its ugly head once again?

The group knew.

We were there together.

First the rabbi quoted Elie Wiesel. Then he read from the Torah, and one by one, the politicians, police chief, pastors, rabbis, and Imams, went to the microphone to say the same thing, again and again: "death will not have the final word today."

Hatred will not rise up unanswered.

The swastika might have been spray painted on our walls and fences, but it has already been painted over by this community's love.

Because of such words, by the time I left, I could see clearly again that as the Apostle Paul said, "While there is evil in the world, evil will be overcome by good. Salvation is nearer to us now than when we first began" for the night is gone, the day is near. However, we must do something in order to remember, and so God gave Moses the instructions.

What we've just read in our second Scripture lesson is more than a story.

It's more than history.

It's interactive.

It's what preachers call liturgy.

What we have in this 12th chapter of the book of Exodus is a way to remember that God is at work in the world. It's a rhythm. It's a process. It's a routine that helps us all to taste and see that God is good. It reminds me of a moment I just read about. I just finished reading a book about a man who drove to a wine bar, drank two bottles, got punched in the face by the bartender, got into his car, was pulled over immediately, refused the breathalyzer, got locked up, had to call his little brother to come pick him up, then he threw up on the way home.

That's a depressing story, isn't it?

It made me want to put on my funeral suit, only in the book, that night at the dinner table, his mother took his face in her hands and said, "You are loved."

That's powerful.

Still, you can imagine what he said.

He said, "Mom, I know."

"No," she says. "You don't know. You won't ever know. And that's okay. It's not your job to know. It's your job to be loved."

After that, the words started to sink in.

That's what it takes, isn't it?

It takes not just the words but hearing them said more than once, plus the motions, the actions, over and over again, year after year, maybe even day after day. It's what should be happening for every child in every family.

I was standing outside a church one afternoon with a public defender in Columbia, Tennessee. She asked, "Do you know what every solid family in this town has in common?" "No, I don't," I admitted. Then she gave a simple, yet profound answer, "Every solid family in this town has a table. Maybe it's a kitchen table. Maybe it's a dining room table. Maybe it's just a card table that they must fold out and sit around, but they do, night after night for the evening meal. I have always known that for a family to stay connected and for children to be reminded that they're loved, there has to be a place where everyone gathers around to be fed, not just in body but in spirit."

Have you ever thought about that?

My friends, it may feel like the darkness is growing out in the world. Hate crimes are up 19% in our country. There's division and discord. Worse still is all the indifference.

I hear people saying, "I'm just done, and what can I do about it anyway?"

What can any of us do about it?

What is there to say?

Every year, God told the people: Gather around, take a lamb, divide it up, eat it together, and remember that I delivered you from oppression in Egypt. Gather around the table, look into the faces of the people whom you love, the people who love you. Feed them, listen to them, and remember the God who provided the food that's there and know that we are never abandoned, nor is our God indifferent to our worries or our suffering.

My friends, there's a table set for us today.

The rules are simple enough.

Maybe how we do it is a little different, but with a little imagination, we all know it's still the same. There's bread and the fruit of the vine. We gather around it together in this very hour as a family of faith, and the One Who set this table for us not only joins us here to serve as Host but gave us everything that we would be fed and saved. "Take and eat," He said, "this is my body given for you. Drink, my blood shed for the forgiveness of sins."

Do these things, and know that you are loved.

Do these things and remember the One Who will conquer all, defeating the powers of sin and death, risen to rule the world.

In these troubled times, do not forget that while history may repeat itself, so does deliverance. Thanks be to God.

Amen.

Do Not Be Afraid, Stand Firm, and See
Romans 14: 7-12 and Exodus 14: 5-14
Preached on September 13, 2020

In the middle of a crisis, no one naturally knows what to do. Sometimes, our natural impulse to run makes things worse, so our children are taught to, "stop, drop, and roll" if their clothes catch on fire, and if they come across a gun, they're told, "don't touch, run away, and tell a grown up." That's what we teach our children to do, but then, the second a snowflake falls, we buy out the grocery store.

How long have we been buying out the grocery store now?

During this pandemic, our natural impulses may be doing more harm than good.

I read an article by a Mississippian named Matthew Magee in a magazine called *Okra* (not the person, the vegetable). He wrote that on March 15th:

My adrenaline kicked in and off I went to the local grocery store with the intent of stocking up on essentials and all manner of junk food. I may have overreacted by buying a 25 lb. bag of rice which is still sitting in my pantry... I remember telling myself to calm down and quit being so dramatic. Words of wisdom from Mister Rogers came to me, "When I was a boy and I would see scary things in the news, my mother would say to me, 'Look for the helpers. You will always find people who are helping'." So that's what I did. I went to the helper aisle – the Hamburger Helper aisle, that is. I stood there observing all the variety boxes of Hamburger Helper with the wonderful childhood mascot Lefty, the Helping Hand, smiling back at me... I started thinking that this shelter in place was meant to flatten the curve of COVID-19 not fatten the curves to gain 19.

We all did some version of that back in March.

Now it's September.

For many of us, this has been one long six months of persistent panic and anxiety. For others, there's been illness and worry about those who are sick. Some have lost loved ones without being able to have a funeral. Then for others, there's boiling-over frustration with a disease that on the one hand, causes no worse symptoms than the common cold, while on the other hand, has killed nearly 200,000 Americans. My friends, we're still in the midst of a crisis we don't know how to deal with.

On this special Sunday, when we remember our Presbyterian roots in Scotland, celebrating tradition and heritage, let us look back on our legacy of faith to learn from one great hero who faced a far worse crisis that we might gain some perspective on the one we face today. Let us look to Moses, who stood among the panicked Israelites with peace of mind even as the Egyptians were on their heels.

I can almost see him.

He led them out of Egypt just days before.

Then, as the Egyptian horde approached, Moses stood there with his feet in the sand, for on the one side was the army and on his other side was the sea. I imagine the waves were breaking against his knees while the Egyptians were breathing down his neck, and it wasn't just a few of them; it was six hundred hand-picked chariots, plus all the others. As though he weren't merciless already, Pharaoh's heart was hardened. He told his army to charge, determined to stop at nothing to bring his source of free labor back to the mines or brick factories, even if he had to kill half of them first. This is a terrifying situation for any leader to find himself in, only to make matters worse, the Israelite people cried out to Moses, "Why have you taken us out here? To die in the wilderness? Were there not enough graves in Egypt? Is that why you took us out here?"

I can understand their panic.

They were unarmed, untrained, and on foot.

You can imagine the chariots circling on one side, the ocean on their other. These people were pinned in, before and behind, asking: "Where is there to turn? Where is there to go? What are we to do?" In response to their panic, Moses said to the people, "Do not be afraid, stand firm, and see… See the deliverance that the Lord will accomplish for you today; for the Egyptians whom you see today you shall never see again. The Lord will fight for you, and you have only need to keep still."

Do you know how counterintuitive that kind of advice is?

It's right, but it calls us to do something contrary to ordinary human behavior.

If we were roasting marshmallows and your sleeve caught on fire, the first thing most people would do is to run. In a panic, we all might run, which would only feed the flame. Likewise, any curious child who comes across a gun will first want to pick it up, with no idea of how powerful it is or how much damage the gun might do. Therefore, we all teach our children from a very young age: stop, drop, and roll. Don't touch, run away, tell a grown up. Why then do we all have 25-pound bags of rice in our pantries and attics filed with toilet paper?

It's because, like the Israelites before us, when we get afraid, we all have voices inside our heads that say, "Don't just stand there; do something!" However, "Don't just stand there; do something!" only clears out the grocery store shelves, and rushing to reopen only fills up the hospitals, for neither panic nor denial will get us out of this, so first, Moses told the people, "Do not be afraid."

The Bible commands us, "Do not fear," or "Do not be afraid," enough times for every day of the year. That's right, about 365 times Scripture tells us to conquer our fears. Why? It's because people who are afraid give up too easily. They play into the enemy's hand because they quit before they've even tried. Think about it.

Young men who fear rejection never ask the pretty girls out on dates.

Little girls who are scared of spending the night away from home miss out on summer camp.

The one who takes the game-winning shot can't let fear get the best of her or the game is already over. The one who takes a good look at the situation without allowing it to throw her into a panic will take a breath and let the ball fly.

Denial makes us like sheep led to the slaughter.

Fear helps us quit, keeps us quiet, and holds us captive.

Either way, should we deny the facts or allow them to terrify us, we're right where the Evil One wants us: ignorant, foolish, then sick; or hopeless, silent, and easy to control. "Do not fear," Moses said to the people. Why? Because fear would have them surrender before the real journey to freedom had even started. Worse than that, fear would have put them all right into the hands of Pharaoh and blinded them to what was about to happen next.

In a time like this one, we can't be afraid.

Do you think scared men wear kilts? No! We can't be afraid, or we'll give up when the vaccine could be here tomorrow. We can't be afraid because the sea may open up right before us. We can't be afraid because fear gives Pharaoh too much power. More than that, we can't be afraid because scared people run.

"Stand firm," Moses told the people.

"Don't run. Don't just do something. Don't panic. Stand firm."

Did you know that lions roar in the hopes of scattering the heard so that they can gang up on the one separated from the rest? Together and unified, the prey can defend themselves, but if fear has them separating and isolating then it's over. So it is with us. In this moment of crisis, the partisan divide grows worse. Of course, it does. In a state of panic, we long for easy answers and scapegoats, rather than things like compromise or discussion, which take too long.

People cry out:

"Someone needs to do something!"

"What if it's the wrong thing?"

"Who cares!"

That is what some say, only this is a time for standing firm and staying together, for we will not live to see what happens next if we turn on each other now.

Those who seek easy answers or for someone to blame have abandoned their principles. Rather than lose ourselves as they have, let us stand firmly on who God calls us to be, defining ourselves by that high standard of "love your neighbor as yourself."

"Do not be afraid, stand firm, and see," Moses said.

"See what?" I can hear the people ask.

"Who knows?" would have been Moses' answer because it could be anything, for God's hand will not be confined by our feeble imaginations. We only know the shape of the miracle after it's been revealed, so what Moses' example demands of us today is that we simply be open to God doing once again what He promised He would.

Do you believe it?

The choir just sang:

I believe in the sun even when it's not shining.

I believe in love even when I don't feel it.

I believe in God even when God is silent.

That's what life demands of us today. Some would call it faith, and for generations and generations, such a legacy has been passed down to us. On this Sunday, when we remember our roots in Scotland, I don't care if you're

Scottish or not. Regardless of your genetics, follow the example of faithful people like Moses. Take on the legacy of Scotland as though you were the granddaughter of William Wallace. Remember that the Queen of England feared the prayers of that great Scottish Presbyterian John Knox more than all the assembled armies of Europe. Know that ours is a legacy of stubborn defiance and unrelenting hope, for while England outlawed bagpipes, kilts, and the native language of our fore parents, they snuck in patches of their family's plaid tartans to be blessed by God, longing for His blessing more than they feared any human power who tried to keep them down. When we hear those notes that opened our worship service that make up that great anthem "Scotland the Brave," may your blood boil at those who have hid from us the truth, believing nothing could be done, for we are never powerless, nor are we helpless in the face of overwhelming adversity. Ours is a God Who divided the sea. Ours is the mighty God Who is working His purpose out, even now. Do not be afraid, stand firm, and see.

Amen.

Who is Holding Up Your Arms?
Philippians 2: 1-13 and Exodus 17: 1-13
Preached on September 27, 2020

There was a wonderful article in the paper last Sunday written by the Dean of St. Phillip's Cathedral downtown. He's the Very Rev. Samuel G. Candler. (I'd like to know how I might become the Very Rev. Joe Evans, but that's not the point I want to get to.) Living up to his title, this article was very good. It was nearly as good as the one our own Rev. Cassie Waits wrote for the Marietta paper last week, and in it, the Very Rev. Samuel G. Candler claimed that among the long list of essential businesses that we just can't get by without during this pandemic season is the church.

You might not call the church a business, but his argument is that what we do, especially in this hour, is essential; that faith gatherings are essential to life, and not just essential to our spiritual lives. Here's a quote from his article:

By faith gatherings, I do not mean just the transmission of our teaching or our latest social ethic. Teachings and social positions vary, from generation to generation. What is essential about our established religious gatherings is our practice of gathering spiritually with people who are different from us.

Think about it.

"Gathering spiritually with people who are different from us."

How often does that really happen?

This week, we announced a phased reopening for in-person worship to start next Sunday with the first quarter of our congregation being invited. I'm excited about that, though regardless of where or how you worship, whether at home with our virtual service, which will continue, or at the in-person service, which will be a little different (someone said "sanitized") to prevent the spread of the virus, the act of a large group of people doing something together stands in stark contrast to so much of what we've been seeing lately.

This week, we were invited to celebrate our daughter Lily's volleyball season. Her team had to conform to a set of rules, so there were masks and temperature checks. However, the parents who wore masks all ended up on one side, while the parents who didn't want to wear them were on the other side. The ones with their noses sticking out were kind of in the middle. We were all at the same event, but even there, we were divided.

Consider how essential worship is.

When the politicians gather, they are divided by an aisle, but in here, we all gather together to bow our heads before the One God and Father of us all. While different signs decorate our front yards, here we affirm what we all have in common. Churches are filled with different kinds of people who might attend different kinds of rallies, but in this room, we all stand to make one common statement of faith: "I believe in God the Father Almighty, Maker of Heaven and earth." It's a rare thing when a group of people can all agree on one statement about anything, and yet here, in this room, it happens Sunday after Sunday. We do it again and again, week after week, standing all at once to say what we believe.

In our world today, such communal acts are essential. Why? It's because the evil one is doing everything in his power to convince us that we don't have anything in common.

We know now that when we read articles on the Internet, more articles that we might agree with are suggested so that we continue reading what we already agree with without having to read anything that we disagree with. Without exposure to opposing opinions, we build up a kind of false confidence about how wise we are. Therefore, the Very Reverend considers gathering for worship with people we don't agree with to be essential.

Here in this room, we first all stand together and pray a prayer boldly claiming that none of us has it right. This morning, we confessed together using the corporate prayer:

I am too self-righteous for my own good.

Refusing to apologize, I never get beyond my mistakes.

So sure that I'm not broken, I fail to be healed.

Rev. Joe Brice told us that he was worried about leading that prayer because he thought folks would be saying, "Yea, Joe, that sounds about right. You need to be praying that prayer," only I'm the one who wrote it, and I wrote that prayer because I know who I am.

I'm not perfect, but I'm afraid to admit it.

I don't like being wrong, even though I often am.

I'm happy being around people who agree with me; however, I'm worse off when I live in such an echo chamber.

Even more than that, I know that my soul is in jeopardy when there's no one there to disagree with me and save me from myself.

In the words of the Very Reverend:

When we begin to lose… community, our voices become more random and untethered. In fact, we become idiots. Do we know what an idiot is? [We think] an idiot is someone who is dumb or stupid. Instead, the true meaning of the word "idiot" (coming from the Greek, meaning "one's own") is someone who can think only within his or her own mindset, unable to see the world from another's perspective.

Do you know someone like that?

Do you resemble someone like that?

There's a plaque that hangs in our kitchen: *The opinions of the husband in this house do not necessarily represent those of the management.* Our household is blessed by two opinions, two people who make decisions, not always unilaterally. Likewise, today, as we gather for worship, let us rejoice in the truth that we are doing something together and that none of us is perfect, all knowing, or has it all figured out.

This time of worship is something like an A.A. Meeting.

In A.A., the only requirement is admitting that you have a problem you can't fix on your own. In worship, the only requirement is that we admit we have a problem with sin that we can't solve ourselves. There's no shame in admitting such limitations, for even Moses needed help.

There's a bumper sticker: *even Moses started out as a basket case.* Have you seen that one? It's true, and as he grew up, he kept needing a little help. It's there in our second Scripture lesson. Did you notice it?

We've been in Exodus for weeks, both literally and figuratively. We've been reading from the book of Exodus since late August while our lives have been somewhere in between what we once considered normal and what our new normal will become. Something important to remember about the Israelites in the book of Exodus is that while they were out of Egypt but not yet in the Promised Land, they really complained a lot. Last Sunday, Rev. Cassie Waits reflected on how they complained until God provided them with food to eat. That satisfied them for a little while, but now they're thirsty:

From the wilderness of Sin, the whole congregation of the Israelites journeyed by stages, as the Lord commanded. They camped at Rephidim, but there was no water for the people to drink. The people quarreled with Moses and said, "Give us water to drink." Moses said to them, "Why do you quarrel with me? Why do you test the Lord?" But the people thirsted there for water; and the people complained against Moses and said, "Why did you bring us out of Egypt, to kill us and our children and livestock with thirst?"

Maybe that right there is a lesson for us in and of itself.

How many miracles had they received by this time?

There were ten full-on plagues in Egypt, God divided the water of an entire sea, provided food for them out of thin air, and still they complained. If your kids are whiny, they're probably not half as ungrateful as the Israelites were. These Israelites complained and complained and complained, so Moses cried out to the Lord, "What shall I do with this people?" But the Lord said to Moses (and this is what I really want to emphasize), "Go on ahead of the people, and take some of the elders of Israel with you… Strike the rock, and water will come out of it, so that the people may drink."

Maybe you've heard this story before of Moses striking the rock and God again providing this complaining people with exactly what they were asking for, but have you ever noticed that Moses wasn't allowed to go strike the rock alone? Then, when Amalek came and fought with Israel, Moses sent out Joshua to choose some men to go and fight. Whenever Moses raised up his hands, Joshua and the troops would prevail, while when Moses lowered his hands, Amalek prevailed, so:

They took a stone and put it under him, and he sat on it. Aaron and Hur held up his hands, one on one side, and the other on the other side; so his hands were steady until the sun set. And Joshua defeated Amalek and his people with the sword.

Did you hear that?

Even Moses couldn't do it on his own.

He had to take elders with him out to strike the rock. He needed Aaron and Hur to hold up his hands. Why then do some Republicans think that our country will be better if we get rid of all the Democrats, and why do some Democrats think that we'll have achieved utopia once all the Republicans are out of office?

Why do we all have at least one person in our lives who we hope won't show up at Thanksgiving dinner?

Why do we seek uniformity?

Why do we fear disagreements?

Why are we so sure we have it right, and they have it wrong?

It's because we all suffer from self-righteousness.

We all want to do it all on our own.

However, there's only One in human history Who could have, and He chose not to.

Our second Scripture lesson from the book of Philippians says it this way:

Do nothing from selfish ambition or conceit, but in humility regard others as better than yourselves. Let each of you look not on your own interests, but to the interests of others. Let the same mind be in you that was in Christ Jesus, who, though he was in the form of God, did not regard equality with God as something to be exploited, but emptied himself, taking the form of a slave, being born in human likeness.

Did you hear that?

I could complain about the state of our union today so much that you would mistake me for an Israelite, so let me just say this: there's a lot to be worried about these days. We have a lot of work to do, and may that work begin with us, all trying to look more like Him and less like the world.

Last week, I opened up a fortune cookie, and there on the slip of paper, I read: "You would do well to work as a team in the coming weeks." After the week I've had, I know for a fact that I wouldn't have made it had it not been exactly that way. So many people are holding my arms up. Far too many for me to think for a minute that I can pastor this church all on my own, but what about you?

Who is holding your arms up?

Who is keeping your world from falling apart?

Who is delivering your *Amazon* packages, keeping your lights on, changing your sheets, doing your laundry, cutting your grass, paving your road, or stocking your grocery shelves?

Who is saving you from yourself?

Who confronts you when you're wrong?

Who stops you before you run right off that cliff?

Who has given you enough grace to cover up all those broken places?

No one is an island, so accept the help He provides and the accept the truth that we all need each other.

Amen.

The Golden Calf Takes and Takes and Takes
Philippians 4: 1-9 and Exodus 32: 1-14
Preached on October 11, 2020

It's really something what people will get into when left to their own devices, isn't it?

Every parent knows it.

Every teacher knows it.

Every dog owner knows it.

Moses turns his back, and then, "But I've only been gone for a few minutes, and this is what you've done!" You can't turn your back on people. You can't turn your back on children, dogs, grown-ups, or anyone. That's just the way that it is, so I think glitter should be outlawed.

Don't you?

Have you ever had that experience with glitter? If you don't supervise children with glitter, you'll find it in your underwear. I was standing around lacrosse practice yesterday, and a mother told me that her daughter had emptied out a bottle of glitter and a bag of kitty-litter on their floor. She'll be finding little surprises around her house years from now because when people are left alone with glitter or anything else, you had better give them firm instructions or they'll just start doing something, and that something is almost certainly not going to do them or you any long-term good.

Left alone, we just get into too much trouble, and we waste too much time.

I saw the most effective advertising campaign that I've ever seen the other day. It's for an app you can get on your phone called *Duolingo*. It's been helping me learn Spanish, but what got me was their slogan: "In 15 minutes a day you can learn a second language. What is 15 minutes of social media going to get you?"

Not all of you spend time on social media.

The main one is *Facebook*, but there are several tools for keeping up with your friends and spying on your children out there. They're all a great way to share vacation photos, and they can be a great way for people to stay connected in this season of almost forced isolation, though they can also be a really big waste of time, or worse.

Someone said, "I have an app on my phone that tells me which of my relatives are racist. It's called *Facebook*." That's a funny joke because people post their opinions and their thoughts right there on *Facebook* for anyone to see, and some of their opinions and thoughts should never have seen the light of day.

People need supervision.

Moses shouldn't have left them alone.

Look at all the trouble they got into.

When the people saw that Moses delayed to come down from the mountain, the people gathered around Aaron, and said to him, "Come, make gods for us…for this Moses, the man who brought us up out of the land of Egypt, we do not know what has become of him." [So, then] Aaron said to them, "Take off your gold rings and bring them to me." He took the gold from them, formed it in a mold, and cast an image of a calf; and they said, "These are your gods, O Israel, who brought you up out of the land of Egypt!"

This is the strangest thing in the world for people to do; still, it's what we all keep doing again and again and again. We run out of things to do so we get up to something, and that something is not necessarily good for us or anyone else.

I've been reading a book by Bill Bryson about growing up in the 50's. He wrote that television wasn't any good back then. There might only be two or three channels, so he'd have to entertain himself.

Long periods of the day were devoted to just seeing what would happen – what would happen if you pinched a match head while it was still hot or made a vile drink and took a sip of it or focused a white-hot beam of sunlight with a magnifying glass on your Uncle Dick's bald spot while he was napping.

Moses left the Israelites alone, and so they find something to do. Likewise, with a few minutes to spare, some of us scroll through social media on our phones, others start thinking about how nice it would be to get out on the lake in our own boat. Our minds wander, we get distracted, as my friend James Fleming always says: "there are 24 hours in a day, and you have to fill them with something," only here's the thing, what's the return on how we are spending our time?

How does scrolling through your friend's vacation pictures make you feel after 15 minutes? Have you heard the expression: "The two happiest days for a boat owner are the day he buys it and the day he sells it."?

We're all looking for something to do.

We all keep shopping for something.

But what have we found?

What does the Golden Calf give in return for our gold?

That's the question that must be asked, for on the other hand:

God delivered the people from slavery in Egypt.

He divided the sea so that they could walk through on dry land.

When they were hungry, God provided them manna.

Thirsty, God made water come out of a rock.

As they looked for direction, God provided them with Ten Commandments, but what do they do when Moses turns his back for just a minute?

Our God gives and gives and gives, but we wander away to spend our time doing what we shouldn't. Knowing that's just human nature, I urge you to ask yourself: what is the return on all your hobbies and vices? Our God delivers, forgives, and fills the emptiness in our souls. What about that vacation home?

What about all those devices?

Where are you putting your energy?

On what are you spending your money?

And are you getting a good return on your investment?

Last week, I heard Cassie's sermon twice. I thought it was brilliant each time I heard it, especially this line: "from the laws, we learn the character of the Law Maker," and from the laws that God provided, from the Ten Commandments that Moses brought down from the mountain, we see that God is in a relationship with us so that we might thrive, prosper, and never again suffer under the weight of slavery to anything. Why then do we keep on bowing down before golden claves and new pharaohs, believing their empty promises and expecting them to deliver us when we already know Who has set us free?

It's a foolish thing to go looking for happiness in a boat.

It's a foolish thing to go looking for connection through social media.

It's a foolish thing to expect deliverance from a politician.

But we keep doing it.

We keep doing all of it because when we're left to our own devices, we do strange and foolish things. Glitter just gets all over the place, or worse. In this consumer culture of ours, people spend money that they don't have. Why? It's because someone told them that money would buy them happiness, and they believed it.

In our celebrity culture, some place superhuman expectations on the shoulders of mere mortals. Why? They do it because of their campaign promises, which we never should have believed.

This is campaign season for some of the politicians in our church, and what I want them to know is that I'm praying for them because they are taking on a role of absolute servanthood. On the other hand, the ones who make being a politician look bad have forgotten that they were elected to serve the people, not manipulate them.

Remember then to ask: who are you serving and what are you getting in return?

I've told you about a man who bought acres and acres of land out west. He made all this money so he could get away from it all. He built this beautiful house way out in the wilderness. His son went to visit him, and he said, "My father has built the most beautiful prison the world has ever seen."

We keep giving our gold to the Golden Calf, but the Golden Calf can't give us anything in return. Do you know that?

The Lord Who delivered us from Egypt tells us to give 10% of what we have away.

Do you know what kind of person actually does that?

Surely, you don't know who gives what to the church, and we shouldn't, but I've met some of the most philanthropic people, so now I know how to spot them.

You'll be able to spot them, too, if you know what to look for.

Think of the most joyful person you've ever met.

Think of the person who always has a smile on her face or a spring in his step.

Think of the one who never complains and who exudes hope.

That's the person who's giving away her money to something good rather than laying it at the feet of a golden calf.

The Golden Calf makes empty promises and is glad to take your gold. His priests have these great big billboards from here to Chattanooga: buy an RV and have a happy family, buy a boat and set yourself free, buy happiness, buy joy, buy fulfillment. It won't work.

Some people spend more money on cable TV than they give to the church.

What's the return on that investment?

The Golden Calf will take your money while offering sitcoms in return. On the other hand, the real God keeps saying, "give it away and find joy."

Guess what, it works every time.

I think about the movie *Schindler's List*. Do you remember what he does at the end of that movie? At the end of that movie, he sees that there's a ring on his finger, a gold ring, and he says, "How many people could this have saved?"

It's so strange what people will do with gold.

Before you spend your next dollar, be sure to think about what you're getting in return because the golden calf takes and takes and takes without giving anything back to your soul, but what about God?

Our God is faithful to us.

Our God has proven himself to us.

So why don't we listen?

It reminds me of a new minister who was trying to enter the Presbytery of Middle Tennessee. Before a new minister can serve a church in a new presbytery, he or she must be examined on the floor in front of every other minister and so many elders. Some of the questions they get asked are hard to answer, others are easier. At some point or another, every new minister trying to enter the Presbytery of Middle Tennessee will be asked as this one was, "Do you love Jesus?" The new pastor was nervous, but with confidence he said, "Yes, I do, but not nearly as much as He loves me."

There's a lot to balance when it comes to your time and your treasure, but I tell you that you must make God your first priority because you are always His.

If you do with what you have according to His commandments, you'll only have more of the joy that He's promised.

Now and finally: *Whatever is true, whatever is honorable, whatever is just, whatever is pure, whatever is pleasing, whatever is commendable, if there is any excellence and if there is anything worthy of praise, think about these things. Keep on doing the things that you have learned and received and heard and seen, and the God of peace will be with you.*

Now and forever, Amen.

In the Cleft of the Rock
1 Thessalonians 1: 1-10 and Exodus 33: 12-23
Preached on October 18, 2020

The Scripture lessons you've just heard remind me of a song we used to sing in Sunday school and then in youth group. I feel sure you're familiar with it. It's based on Matthew chapter 7, and it goes like this:

Seek ye first the kingdom of God,

And his righteousness,

And all these things shall be added unto you,

Allelu-, alleluia.

That's the chorus. The verse I'm really thinking of after reading this Scripture lesson from the book of Exodus is the second or third one:

Ask and it shall be given unto you,

Seek and ye shall find.

Knock and the door shall be opened unto you,

Allelu-, alleluia.

We used to sing that with Vivian Stephens, who died during this epidemic, and while we haven't yet been able to remember her at a funeral, I'll always remember her when I think of that song or the many others she taught us to sing. "Seek Ye First" is what we called it, and it's wonderful to sing in a round, yet the reason I think of it now is because it calls us never to settle, but to ask. That's what Moses did.

He dared ask to see God.

That was a bold thing to do, especially when you think about how easy it is to settle.

When I was a kid, it was easy to settle because we didn't always know what else was out there. For example, every once in a while, back when we were kids, maybe once a month or so, my mom wouldn't be home for dinner because she'd be meeting with her book club. When that happened, my father was in charge of feeding us supper, which made supper interesting.

I don't know what it meant in your family, but for my sister, brother, and me, our father cooking supper meant that he'd drive us to Ingle's grocery store on

Powder Springs Road. Then he'd lead us to the sardines, where he'd say, "Pick out whatever can you want!"

Could we have asked for something else for supper?

I don't know. I never thought to ask.

Could we have maybe asked that he take us out to our favorite Mexican restaurant, which was right across the street, or maybe even to Chuck E. Cheese, where a kid can be a kid? I don't know because no one ever asked. We were offered sardines, and we were thankful to have them. That sounds like the right attitude for children to have, doesn't it?

Have you ever wished that your children or grandchildren would just appreciate all that they have already? Have you ever avoided running into Target with them just because you don't want to hear them asking for more? I do all the time, only Scripture keeps pushing us and them not to settle, but to ask.

Ask and it shall be given unto you,

Seek and ye shall find.

Knock and the door shall be opened unto you.

Those are the words of Jesus, and more than that, all the really annoying people who won't stop asking for what they want or can't help but fight for what they believe in, rather than paint them as annoying, entitled, or ungrateful, Scripture remembers them as good examples of how we should all be.

Think about it: there's the Canaanite woman who won't settle for the scraps that fall from the table, but boldly calls on Jesus to heal her daughter, and the Lord does. There's the parable of the widow who returns, day after day, to the unjust judge until she receives justice. What does Jesus say about her? He said, "Will not God grant justice to his chosen ones who cry to him day and night?" so now consider Moses, who says to God, "Show me your glory, I pray."

What a bold request.

Have you ever asked God for something like that?

Surely, I never have.

I've never even had to audacity to expect to be treated like a human being when I call our Internet company, much less call on God for any more than I have already. Yet, consider the song:

Ask and it shall be given unto you,

Seek and ye shall find.

Knock and the door shall be opened unto you.

Don't settle.

Keep going.

Keep asking.

Keep pushing.

We're on our way to something more, so fight for it. That's what it takes.

According to legend, George Frederic Handel, whom Beethoven considered the greatest composer who ever lived, wrote his most famous piece, *Messiah*, in 24 days. After completing the most famous portion of *Messiah*, the "Hallelujah" chorus, he is reported to have said to a servant either, "I did think I did see all Heaven before me, and the great God himself," or "I thought I saw the face of God."

Certainly, we never would have made it to the moon had humanity been satisfied just staring up at it. Presbyterian astronaut John Glenn gave reporters an idea of what it's like in outer space: "To look out at this kind of creation and not believe in God is to me impossible."

What does it take then to catch a glimpse of the divine, as they did?

What is required to see, if not God's face, then a sliver of His glory?

I tell you, first of all, we are required to ask, though just that is hard for a lot of people to do. Sometimes, I'll meet with couples before they get married. Maybe she'll tell me that he never considers her opinion. Then I'll ask, "Does he know what your opinion is? Have you told him?" That's a good place to start. Maybe he wouldn't listen anyway, but that's a good place to start because talking with your mother about him probably isn't going to change anything.

I've been reading the paper a lot lately, and it has me thinking about how sometimes, it's like we're afraid to ask directly, like maybe we're afraid to say what it is that we really want in the presence of those who might give it to us.

An old newspaper man named Sam Kennedy, who ran the local paper back in Tennessee, once told me, "If you want to know the true nature of your community, always read the letters to the editor." There, in our local Marietta paper, I've been reading about all kinds of stuff. Lately, I've read about political yard signs getting stolen or vandalized; months ago, it was frustration with the local schools not opening their classrooms for in-person learning. My general reflection based on many of these letters to the editor is that we are a society who has such trouble talking with people who think differently that we use forums like the "letters to the editor" section of the paper as a way to vent because we're too scared to talk with each other face to face.

Now, Dan Kirk never vents like that in his letters to the editor.

I don't know if you ever read what he writes, but you should. Interestingly, our own Dan Kirk just writes in to remind us to be grateful for how lucky we are, but that's beside the point.

By and large, I believe we settle for venting to the newspaper when we could be speaking our concerns to the people who could do something about it.

When I think of such behavior, I worry that we're settling for ranting when we could be moving forward. We wind up feeling helpless and frustrated when we could be working for a brighter future. We grow used to yelling and finger-pointing and call it governance. We allow our neighbors to do as they please, even when it drives us crazy because it's easier to go back inside to watch TV than to ask them to put on a mask, turn down their music, or just come over for dinner.

Why do we go back to watching TV; why do we put our heads down, minding our own business, when we could be asking for more? We'd never have gotten to the moon if we hadn't learned to work together, and we'll never make it to the Promised Land if we don't start moving towards each other now.

That's why I think the most important quote of all when it comes to glimpsing the divine as Moses, Handel, or John Glenn did is that of Victor Hugo, the playwright of *Les Misérables*, who is reported to have said, "to love another person is to see the face of God."

Maybe that's the greatest frontier.

Maybe that's the place where so many of us end up settling for less.

It's so hard to love someone. It requires nearly everything of us. Think about Moses. He killed the Egyptian and lost his home in the palace. Why? Because he loved his people.

He left his home in the wilderness to answer a call from God to set his people free. Why? Because he couldn't bear the thought of their suffering.

He faced Pharaoh with nothing more than a staff in his hand.

He led them out of slavery and through the waters of the sea, just trusting that God would provide a way.

They got hungry, and he was bold to ask for food.

They got thirsty, and he was bold to ask for water.

They kept complaining about him, and he was bold to ask God to love them anyway.

Love kept pushing him to do more and to be more, even though they were like five-year-olds on a long road trip, even though every five minutes one had to stop and use the bathroom.

On this long road trip that lasted 40 long years, so long that even God had had enough, saying to Moses, "I will not go up among you [to the Promised Land], or I would consume you on the way, for you are a stiff-necked people," Moses says to the Lord, "Please, stay with us."

"And just let me see your glory."

You know what we settle for?

We settle for living in a country with people we don't agree with.

We settle for getting along with neighbors whom we can't understand and who might be stealing our political yard signs.

We settle for putting up with, tolerating, just getting through this election without ringing someone's neck, but do you know what the Gospel demands of us? Love your neighbor as yourself.

The time has come to ask for more out of our country, who made it to the moon years ago, but today can't seem to engage in civil discourse.

The time has come to ask more from ourselves, who can read about what's happening all around the world, but don't always know what's happening across the street.

The time has come for us to ask more of our neighbors, who may need to be reminded that while we are free to do all kinds of things, we are never free to hate.

With boldness, let us dare ask for more. In doing so, if we do so out of love, we'll see the face of God.

Amen.

But You Shall Not Cross Over There
1 Thessalonians 2: 1-8 and Deuteronomy 34: 1-12
Preached on October 25, 2020

What do you think was going through his mind up on Mount Nebo? What do you think Moses thought as the Lord showed him the whole land, the great plains, palm trees, and the flowing river Jordan? It was that land flowing with milk and honey that he had been looking forward to seeing. Up on the mountain, he looked over into it. Surely it was with tears in his eyes that he heard the Lord saying, "This is the land of which I swore to Abraham, to Isaac, and to Jacob." This is what you've been dreaming of.

This is what you've been looking forward to.

This is the vision that's been keeping you going.

Now you see it, "But you shall not cross over there."

What did that feel like?

The feeling that comes to mind from my personal experience, albeit incredibly minor in comparison, is what I felt at the end of my hardest week as a camp counselor. I was a camp counselor for one summer up at Camp Cherokee on Lake Allatoona. My sister still loves that place, maybe more than any other place on earth, but for me, I was always happy to be there while also being happy to go back home once each session was over. That was especially true after the hardest session of the summer. This one week was with middle schoolers. Middle schoolers are hard enough, but these were serious-about-camping middle schoolers, who actually chose to sleep in tents for the whole week, away from running water and electricity.

We were a mile or so away from the main camp.

We cooked all our own food.

We lived in the wild, and when it was finally over, I was ready to go home, so ready that I could taste it. I sat down in my car with such relief at the thoughts of a hot shower and my own bed, only my car wouldn't start.

Do you know that feeling?

You say to yourself, "It's finally over," but fate or bad luck or God says, "No, it's not."

Why does that happen?

What are we supposed to learn from something like that?

Doesn't it make it easier to do hard things if there is a promise of receiving a blessing in the end? What changes in your life if you accept the truth that the outcome is not guaranteed? Sometimes we act as though it were.

Have you ever worked overtime in expectation of a promotion that never came?

Are you pushing through this time of quarantine with the hope that a vaccine will be here in March? Guess what, there's no guarantee, so we must ask: had Moses known he would never cross over into the Promised Land, would he still have left Egypt? It's sort of like asking, "Would you have moved to New Zealand back in April if you knew it was going to take us so long to get our acts together?" Or thinking of not our present, but our history, "What was going on in the mind of the first 12 members of First Presbyterian Church who started meeting in an old log house in November of 1835?"

Would they have left their established homes and already-built churches to break ground right here had they known what it was really going to be like?

Had someone told them about raids, droughts, and dysentery would they have laid the foundation that we now stand on?

They were but four families who started this church: the Mayeses, the Simpsons, the Hamiltons, and the Lemons. Leonard Simpson was one of our two first elders. He also ran the local tavern, and he died in 1856 at the age of eighty-seven, which gave him about three years to worship in the brick sanctuary that wouldn't have been there without him. Just three years to sit in such a beautiful place for worship, a sanctuary built to seat 300 by a congregation that numbered 96 at the time. The land on which it was built was donated by Rev. John Jones, their preacher, only it wasn't finished until after his resignation.

What was that like?

What is it like to work so hard for something, yet never see it come to full bloom?

What is it like to look forward to something that you never see materialize?

What is it like to make sacrifices, not for yourself and your immediate gratification, but for those who come along later, maybe long after your lifetime?

God's story is a long one, but we are like grass. That's a hard truth to accept.

A friend from Tennessee, Neeley King, wrote me a line she read or heard in a sermon, or she's so witty she probably came up with it herself: we live in a microwave society, but we have a crockpot God. That's a hard truth to live with, maybe especially for her husband John, who used to let me know that the service was running too long by putting down his hymnal, waving his arms, and pointing to his wristwatch from his pew in the back.

Like him, we're an impatient people.

Scripture calls us to be patient all the time, yet we can do all our Christmas shopping online, and it will be on our doorsteps by the end of the week. People say, "Rome wasn't built in a day," but ask a contractor how many customers patiently wait for their renovations to be complete. The truth about humanity is that we want it now. We love immediate gratification, while so much of what we have, so many of the gifts we enjoy, were not thrown together in a moment or even a lifetime but passed down through the generations.

Moses was not permitted to cross over.

After he died, generation after generation has inherited his blessing.

So "The Israelites wept for Moses in the plains of Moab thirty days."

If you can see today's worship bulletin, that's what's painted on the cover. For thirty days the Israelites wept for Moses because he had brought them so far and had given them so much, yet he died before his feet could touch the Promised Land.

Does that make you sad?

It does me, only not too sad if I think about it this way: a friend of mine named Roben Mounger has a rug in her house. Her grandmother started it for her when she was just a little girl. She wanted it to be in her granddaughter's home when she grew up, which must have seemed to little Roben, at the time, as a future so far away that it would never get here. She was just a child, and what is having her own house to a little girl other than a far-off dream? Christmas takes forever to get here when you're young. When you're young, you're so short-sighted that you turn a crank to make ice-cream, but it feels like ice cream might never happen. Still, it does happen, and in Roben's house is the rug her grandmother made her. Her grandmother died before she ever saw it in there, but is a piece of her grandmother not with her always?

Our daughter Lily is named after my grandmother.

My paternal grandmother painted with oils, and still, whenever I smell them, it's like I'm in her house again. Some of her artwork hangs in our house, and

I point them out to Lily, saying, "Your great-grandmother, whom you're named after, painted that, and she would have loved you."

What does it mean to pass something like that down?

What does it mean to invest in something so far into the future?

I tell you, it's this great act of faithful giving that helps us to remember that there will be a future. This year, we're completing the final phases of that capital campaign you funded two years ago. We're working to expand the playground on Church Street. Do you know the one I'm talking about? Do you know how good it is to think about expanding that playground? Do you know how good it makes me feel to think about kids playing on it without having to wear face masks? Someday it will happen.

Someday, it's going to be better than it is right now.

Someday, we're going to look back on this moment, and we'll tell those who can't remember what it was like, "Yes, we really did have to wear masks. Yes, the restaurants could only do take out. Yes, the toilet paper really was all gone. Yes, we were scared, but we made it. We made it, and now, look where we are."

Moses knew where he was going, and even though he never reached it himself, I know that he died a happy man because a congregation of 96 people built a Sanctuary that can now seat 300. Four families were so determined to have a Presbyterian Church in Marietta, Georgia that now we have this place and each other. Just the idea that our children might have a better life fills me with so much joy I can't help but smile because while I might not step into the future with them, knowing they will have a better future gives me hope.

What we do today ensures that this church will be an institution that will outlive us all, and that won't be true for all churches. Some have said that one in five will close during this pandemic, yet I know that from this pulpit, the Gospel will be proclaimed by preachers who haven't even been born yet. And that from their heavenly home, the generations who came before us will rejoice knowing that this church that they invested in will be a home to their descendants in the faith, for while we are the stewards of this great legacy, we are building on what they started. Today, I'm asking you to take your pledge card and to make an investment in the future.

Why?

So we will make it another year?

Sure.

More precisely, though, so we can pass the gift of this great place down to the coming generation better than we found it, which is fitting, for it's because of this place that we are better now than when He found us. Isn't that right?

Who was I when I wandered into this church as a 3rd grade kid? Who was I when I stacked bricks on a mission trip to Mexico as a high schooler? Tim Hammond, who was there on my first trip with our youth group, reminded me that, inspired by our bad behavior, the van my friends and I rode in down to Mexico was nicknamed "The Paddy Wagon" by all the adult advisors. Well, I've gone from the Paddy Wagon to the Pulpit, and it's because the Gospel I heard here has made me better than I was.

How then can I not want to leave this place in better shape than I found it?

We increased our pledge this year.

Why?

It's because we've been blessed by this place, and the blessing of this place must be preserved for those kids who would be in the nursery.

Will you help keep it going for their children and our children's children?

For I tell you that as this day turns into the next, and as the far-off tomorrow turns into the day after that, how we live now will resound through a future we'll never set foot in. They'll remember, though, the gift they received, and we will rest knowing we left this place better than we found it.

Presbyterians are weird about money.

We don't like to talk about it, so I'm just going to say it as plainly as I can: Everything you have comes from God, and in Scripture we are called to give 10% of what we have away. Take your pledge card and invest a portion of what you have into this church and her bright, ongoing future. Not only will this church be stronger and better for you having done so, but you will be stronger, better, and more hopeful for having done so.

Amen.

From All Saints' to Advent

This next sermon was preached on All Saints' Sunday, a Sunday for remembering all those who died in the last year. In a sense, this holy day was more important to me the year I preached it than it's ever been before because so many whose loved ones were remembered on All Saints' Sunday 2020 hadn't been able to have funerals, at least not the kind of funerals they would have liked to have had.

Still, I remember the season in which I preached these sermons as a hopeful time. From All Saints' Sunday, we moved into the season of Advent, that great time of anticipation where we prepare ourselves for the coming of Christ. We were preparing ourselves for so much – we were hoping for a vaccine, for our kids to go back to school, to worship again in person, to travel outside our homes, and so much more. Thanks be to God, hope for us is not just a fantasy but a reality Who comes to us in human form.

Who Are These?
1 John 3: 1-3 and Revelation 7: 9-17
Preached on November 1, 2020

Last Sunday, my brother was in town, and we were all having lunch outside after church at McAlister's by the hospital. We were discussing etiquette and appropriate wardrobe for *Zoom* meetings. Because he's now an English composition professor at a community college in Charlotte, teaching all his classes online rather than in-person, one of our girls asked him if he ever taught his classes while wearing pj's.

Generally, we agreed that wearing pj's to teach a college class sends the wrong message, but my brother and our girls also thought it would be nice if there were a line of formal pj's that looked sort of like a suit and tie to wear while lecturing a class from home during a pandemic. (If someone takes this idea and runs with it, just tithe back 10% to the church, please.)

My point is that clothes matter this way.

What you have on says a lot about you.

I once met a pastor who had served great big churches in great big cities, and I asked him, "What should I be working on as I prepare for a life in ordained ministry?" Thinking he might emphasize a healthy prayer life or a disciplined routine for studying Scripture, instead he looked at my outfit and told me to shine my shoes. "People judge you by what you wear. If you want people to think that you're taking ministry seriously, show them by dressing seriously." That's what he said, and I think he's right about that. I've challenged myself to live by that advice, and I've repeated his words more than once, only consider what the saints were wearing.

We've just read a beautiful passage of Scripture from the book of Revelation. I believe it's this passage that inspired the hymn, "When the Saints Go Marching In." Here in Revelation is this great multitude, made up of all tribes and peoples and languages.

Surely, we all want to be in that number, but what does it take?

What is required?

Do you have to shine your shoes to be one of the saints in light?

No, that's not it.

Notice what they're wearing.

Their wardrobe is explained by one of the elders: "These are they who have come out of the great ordeal; they have washed their robes and made them white in the blood of the lamb."

Their wardrobe says a lot about them, though what their white robes mean isn't necessarily obvious, so let me try and clarify. I always wear white, pressed shirts to lead worship. When I'm getting dressed, I flip up the collar to put on my tie. (This isn't a clip-on.) However, because I'm not very good at shaving, sometimes I'll get a little blood on my collar, and if it's too obvious, I'll put that shirt aside to get another, for in this case, a spot of blood is an imperfection. For them, having been washed in the blood of Christ's sacrifice is their salvation, as His death washes away all imperfection.

His blood makes us clean and new.

It is because He died that we are saved. We are not saved because we are perfect, for we are not, nor could we ever be. Yet so often when we think about being a saint, and oh, how I want to be in that number, we think about being good, pure, steadfast, and holy, only that's not what makes this multitude different. That's not what set them apart.

It's that they've been washed in His sacrifice.

It's that they've accepted His mercy.

It's that they're not waiting until their world is perfect to stop and sing.

They know Who is in control, so even as the sky falls, they're singing praises already.

Notice how they sing.

Notice what they're wearing.

Consider what they've been through.

We read that "These are they who have come out of the great ordeal." What was that? Some might say that we're in the middle of one right now. Some of you are working hard to get out of it, by urging your friends to wear their masks so that this virus gets under control or making sure that your friends vote so that we're either delivered from tyranny or protected from it, depending on your political persuasion. How did they make it through their great ordeal?

You may know that the book of Revelation was written in the time of the Roman Empire, and when the book speaks of evil at work in the world and the rule of the anti-Christ, it's the Roman Empire that Revelation refers to; however, we keep reading this book, hundreds of years after the fall of Rome because Christians in every age must struggle to live in a society that doesn't always reflect the values of Christians.

The question for us today is: what are we to do, and what do we learn from them?

Are we saved once we've fought back all the evil?

Are we saved once we've voted all the right people into office?

Are we saved once we've finally created a holy society and a more perfect union, with shoes shined and clean, white shirts?

Certainly, many act as though this were the case, for some will storm the streets next week if the vote doesn't go their way.

Is that what it takes to be a Saint?

Some of you have voted already. Others of you will vote on Tuesday. I don't feel that it's appropriate for me to tell you whom you ought to vote for. Politics is not my area of expertise; religion is, so I feel qualified to tell you that the one who will be elected might be president, but he's not really in control. Regardless of who wins, he might think he's running the show, but he reports to a Higher Power.

Some think that "if our man wins," everything is going to turn in our favor, and if the other wins, the world will fall apart, while the saints know that Christ has already saved and redeemed them. We must remember that.

Politically, we're a split congregation.

Half of you are going to be disappointed this week.

Some of you are going to watch the results come in, and you'll worry about the future of our nation. Some of you are going to wish your spouse didn't vote for the other guy and cancelled your vote out. If you find yourself devastated on November 5th or whenever all the votes are really counted, the ones who trust only in human power will storm the streets, while the saints among us will remember that God is in control.

If the next president is good, great. Glory to God. But if he's bad, God will still be at work, revealing the sins of our nation and reminding us that we were fools to put so much trust in one mortal.

That's the difference: some of us think the world and the future rests in our hands, while saints are always putting their trust, not in human power, but in God's.

So I hope you'll vote.

I hope you'll vote like the future depends on it because it does, but I also hope you'll sing because God is in control.

I hope you'll stand up for what you believe in because you are powerful, but I also hope you'll kneel to pray because you are not all-powerful.

I also hope you'll choose your candidates and advocate for them, but remember that there's a whole multitude of people up there beyond the Pearly Gates whom we must join, and if we don't get better at unity now, we're going to have a long learning curve once we get to Heaven.

Today, we'll name those of our congregation who joined the ranks of that great multitude this past year. What we'll remember about them is not just what they did or failed to do. All their accomplishments and all their sins are nothing compared to this one commonality: they were washed in the blood of the Lamb. Knowing that He can do for us what we could never do for ourselves, we remember those who have died, not with sorrow only. We'll remember them, knowing that they join that great multitude who has been welcomed into everlasting life because of the power of God.

A man in a former church named Rufus Ross gave me a small booklet full of tips for writing difficult letters. It includes an example for help in writing that most difficult of letters, the acknowledgement at the time of death. Benjamin Franklin wrote this one to a friend who had just lost his son to suicide:

We have lost a most dear and valuable friend. But it is the will of God and nature, that these mortal bodies be laid aside, when the soul is to enter into real life… Death is that way. A mangled painful limb, which cannot be restored, we willingly cut off. He who plucks out a tooth, parts with it freely, since the pain goes with it, and he who quits the whole body parts at once with all pains and possibilities of pains and diseases which it was liable to, or capable of making him suffer. Our friend and we were invited abroad on a party of pleasure, which is to last forever. His chair was ready first, and he is gone before us. We could not all conveniently start together, and why should you and I be grieved at this, since we are soon to follow and know where to find him?

Their chairs were ready first, but we are soon to follow.

Notice their robes and be washed in the blood of the Lamb. Lean not on your own understanding or your own strength, for we are all limited in our understanding and are all fading away like grass. May our legacy be, not what we fought for or held onto, but Whom we trusted.

On Christ the solid Rock, I stand;
All other ground in sinking sand,
All other ground is sinking sand.
Amen.

When the Lights Go Out
1 Thessalonians 4: 13-18 and Matthew 25: 1-13
Preached on November 8, 2020

I asked Lynne Sloop, a great leader in our congregation, how she and her husband, Bob, had weathered the tropical storm that went through Cobb County the week before last. Lynne said they were fine, but she was humbled, as losing electricity always seems to show her that she's a little less self-sufficient than she thought she was.

I liked that response.

I could relate to it because the same was true for us.

We were fine, but we were humbled because that tropical storm forced us to recognize that our lives are a little luxurious compared to how our ancestors lived.

My grandfather was raised in a place called the Caw-Caw Swamp. That's in the Lowcountry of South Carolina. He was born at home in their cabin, premature, so without a NICU to rush him off to, his mother had to make do. She heated bricks in the fire, made a pallet for him on the floor, and stacked the warmed bricks around him, making her own incubator without a hospital or even electricity. On the other hand, Friday before last, when I woke up in a dark house because the power was out, our automatic coffee maker didn't have my coffee waiting for me like usual.

That was hard for me to deal with.

It only takes a power outage to show me that not all my wicks are trimmed and burning. There's not oil in all my lamps. In fact, there weren't even batteries in all my flashlights because I wasn't expecting a storm to come, and I wasn't ready.

Were you ready?

Not everybody is, and that's part of the point with this parable from the Gospel of Matthew:

Then the kingdom of heaven will be like this. Ten bridesmaids took their lamps and went to meet the bridegroom. Five of them were foolish, and five were wise. When the foolish took their lamps, they took no oil with them; but the wise took flasks of oil with their lamps.

It sounds like this is the parable of the Boy Scouts.

The ones who lived by that motto, "Be prepared," were ready. They were wise. The ones who weren't expecting the bridegroom to take so long were left in the dark, for they didn't bring enough oil with them. However, maybe we should cut them some slack. For one thing, He didn't tell them when He would arrive.

Through this parable, He's telling us, "I'm coming. Be ready, but you don't know the time or the hour." Not knowing when does make His arrival hard to prepare for, only life is full of these situations where we walk into the unexpected.

When that happens, some wind up looking prepared, and some are caught on their heels.

It's been that way during the pandemic. Kroger sold out of dried beans and yeast. That's good for them. On the other hand, Jack's New Yorker Deli, one of my favorite lunch spots, is closed. I walked past their storefront last Thursday morning, and it makes me sad to think about how I'll never again taste their outlaw sandwich or their French fries. What's happened during this epidemic has changed our economy, and it seems as though some were ready, and some were not. I was talking with Tom Clarke, who manages investments for a living, about all the new companies who are doing so well. One example is *Zoom*, and who would have thought that there'd need to be a business that allows people to have meetings at home? I don't know who knew we'd need it, but Tom can tell you, they're rich right now because those who end up prepared for unforeseen circumstances profit.

Five of the bridesmaids had oil reserves, and we ought to be happy for them. In fact, we ought to be happy, too, for all the ways our church was prepared for what we're going through right now. Consider the cameras, lights, and all the livestream technology we have in this room.

Looking back to when we asked you to fund the capital campaign to pay for all this stuff, surely some of you thought, "We'll never need all that. Church on the Internet? That sounds crazy!"

In a way, it sounded a little crazy to me, too, but when the quarantine hit back in March, my parent's church up in Bryson City, North Carolina, was busy trying to figure out how to livestream a worship service for the very first time. My dad was buying an iPad to stream the service, and their preacher was all frustrated by being recorded. Me, down here in this place, I was like Benny Hinn. We already had it all together, and when it comes to the worship service, we never really missed a beat.

The unexpected came, but we were ready, kind of like the wise bridesmaids.

Then, the city schools asked us if we'd be willing to help them distribute milk and produce out of our parking lot. A group of ladies started sowing facemasks. More than 200,000 pounds of food and more than 2,000 masks later, I knew that we had become a church in a virtual world, still changing lives with faith, hope and love, but it was the love part that had me worried.

It still does.

Our church motto is, "changing lives with faith, hope, and love;" however, it's hard to love your neighbor if you don't really know your neighbor.

In this world that's already pretty isolating, and now under a pandemic that mandates isolation, I've been worried about how well we could love each other because there are a whole bunch of us who barely know each other.

We asked these folks to become neighborhood group leaders.

Some of them said, "I emailed my group, but none of them wrote me back."

Another said, "I called all ten households in my neighborhood group, but the first three I called all said they're going to a different church."

That makes it hard; only think about how important it is to have connections.

When the power went out, one family in our church called their neighborhood group leader, who invited them to come on over and put everything from their freezer in hers. When the power goes out, it becomes clear that we need each other, only not everyone has someone they can call, so Home Depot has a run on generators, which is fine, so long as Home Depot's open.

This is what happened in the parable:

As the bridegroom was delayed, all of them became drowsy and slept. But at midnight there was a shout, 'Look! Here is the bridegroom! Come out and meet him.' Then all those bridesmaids got up and trimmed their lamps. The foolish said to the wise, 'Give us some of your oil, for our lamps are going out.' But the wise replied, 'No! there will not be enough for you and for us; you had better go to the dealers and buy some for yourselves.' And while they went to buy it, the bridegroom came.

Here's the question that this parable demands we ask: were they foolish because they didn't bring enough oil, or were they foolish because they ran off to the store in the middle of the night? Were they foolish because they weren't prepared, or were they foolish because they panicked? Were they foolish because they looked within themselves and said, "I don't have enough," or were they foolish because they thought they could find what they needed to fill up their lack at the corner store?

I tell you: the Light of the World is coming.

You're not going to need your lamp.

Just don't run away.

He can bring light to all our darkness.

Just don't panic.

Let Him come.

I feel sure that this isn't really a parable just about self-sufficiency because if we could make it through this life by hoarding enough to keep the lights on then what did Christ die for? If all that was required of a disciple was being ready for anything, then we should shut this church down and turn it into a discount mart for end-of-the-world preppers.

My friends, He died for us because He loved us before we were worthy of His love.

He died to save us before we were worth saving.

We baptize little infants because that's what God's love is like. We are all helpless, unprepared, broken down, and lost in the darkness, so I say these bridesmaids who ran off for oil were foolish, not because they weren't prepared; they were foolish because they were ashamed.

They responded to Christ, not with faith, but anxiety.

The Light of the World was running late, and they thought He'd reject them because there wasn't enough oil in their lamps, but what does the Light of the World need with an oil lamp?

We get in so much trouble preparing for a feast, putting our houses in order, trying to look ready, that we keep out the One Who could make us clean.

I was walking around the neighborhood on election night, and I saw, because I'm nosey enough to look in people's windows, that one of my neighbors already has her Christmas tree up. It's as though we're all getting ready early so we can still have the perfect Christmas, but I tell you this, you can buy out Hobby Lobby to deck your every hall, you can pressure your parents into coming into your house even though they're afraid, you can push right through the wall of every restriction put on us to be more prepared for Christmas than you've ever been, but what are all your preparations compared to the reality that the Son of God is born unto us?

The foolish ones were worried about their oil, while the wise ones didn't even need to use it because this God of ours is at work among us, so stop trying so hard to make things perfect.

You don't have to.

Stop trying so hard to make Thanksgiving special. It already is.

Don't miss out on the whole thing by running back and forth to Kroger. There are moments in life that we miss for trying to be completely prepared. Think about how hard people work to get ready for new babies. Every father spends so much time rushing back and forth to Babies "R" Us, it seems like the baby could be walking before the nursery's finished.

I read a great article about thankfulness.

The author confessed:

In my house, as I am sure it is with many others, conversation, as well as anxiety and flat out worry, surrounds the questions about how are we going to reenact all of our Holiday traditions? Can we gather with family and friends? Will we all wear masks right up until the Thanksgiving Turkey is carved and then eat our dinner, keeping appropriate distance from one another? Will we be able to have Christmas Eve Worship without holding our lit candles while we sing Silent Night with our church family? And pretty quickly we find that we have a knot in our stomach that we can't untie, and our frustrations and anxiety grow with every passing moment.

We can't be ready.

We can't be perfectly prepared, so just be present.

God has this under control, so take a breath.

Back to the storm: our power was out. It was on and off for a couple days. There was a great big tree leaning on our power line. However, there were so many other emergencies to deal with, it took two days for the truck to pull up and start working on it. First, it was three of them walking down our road. I saw the tallest of the three, pointing up at the trees to the other two. It really looked like this guy knew what he was doing. After a while, I walked down there to watch, and that tall guy walks up to me, looking at me like he's trying to place my face.

"What do you do for a living?" he asked.

I didn't know why he was asking.

Did he need more help?

Did I look like I could handle a chainsaw, or was he ready for me to get out of the way?

"I'm a preacher," I told him.

"At First Presbyterian Church?" he asked.

It turns out this man, whose crew got our power back on, goes to church with us every Sunday on *Facebook*. His name is Steve Graham. He's married to Janet, whom I met at a Civitan meeting with Elizabeth Manning, and there wewere, standing in the street, face to face.

I kept on thanking him for getting our power back on. Guess what he said, "You just keep preaching. You don't know how much good that does me. I'm glad to repay the favor."

There is plenty of light out there in the world, so stop trying so hard to makeit perfect. Don't try to make this year just like last year, and don't give up because it's not how you imagined it would be. Instead, rest and wait as you are, and let Him do what He does best, for when the lights go out, the Light of the World shows up.

Amen.

Misjudging the Master
1 Thessalonians 5: 1-11 and Matthew 25: 14-30
Preached on November 15, 2020

As you well know, Jesus often taught using parables, and a parable is what we just read.

A parable is one way He helps us to understand heavenly things. By using what we already know something about, like oil and lamps, mustard seeds, rebellious sons, or in this case, slaves, money, investments, and a master, Jesus helps us to understand something that we don't understand, like God, for example.

I just made the statement that we don't understand God.

The thing is, maybe we think we do.

That's why it went so badly with the third slave. He didn't understand what he was to do with what he had been given, nor did he understand the one who gave it.

There were three slaves. Each was given a very large sum of money. What our Bible calls a *talent* was about a year's salary for a day laborer, only remember that these three were slaves. As slaves, they had nothing, so think about what it must have been like to hold all that money. To have had a full salary all at once would have been intoxicating to a person who expected to work a full lifetime without receiving any pay.

Just think about it.

Have you ever been to an old plantation-turned-museum? You go through the big house, and maybe there's furniture and a candelabra. Maybe you see what all the master and his family would have owned: toys in the nursery, glass mirrors, and polished doorknobs. Then you go out to where the slaves' quarters once stood. There are cabins with a dirt floor, maybe a table, a chair, and a pallet in the corner. It's likely that an archaeologist excavated the area to find what's been left by the people who lived there, only all that this archaeologist found was a button, a clay pipe, and a broken glass bottle.

Can you imagine what it would feel like if all you owned in the whole wide world was a glass bottle, but then you're given a full year's wages, times two or even five?

What do you do with all that money?

What do you do with anything so huge that comes into your possession?

Maybe you just hold onto it, without knowing what to do.

That's a problem because it's possible to ruin things by holding on to them too tightly.

Consider the transition of power. We know that democracy works best when politicians remember that their primary task is to serve the people rather than get themselves re-elected, yet so many hold onto their office, as though the point of having political power were maintaining it. They hold onto the talents God has given them too tightly, and so they disappoint the Master. That can happen.

Maybe that's happening right now.

According to the *Atlanta Journal Constitution's* Editorial Board, at least a couple politicians have questioned the integrity of our recent elections without any real evidence. Are they doing our country any favors if they hold onto political power, breaking our trust in the electoral process? Or, thinking of the parable, does the master entrust these slaves with such huge gifts so that they can just hold onto what they've been entrusted with? No. In fact, I believe the parable teaches us that the master desires something much bigger than that.

Two of the slaves risk losing what the master gave them so that what's his flourishes and grows, which makes me think of what's happened here in Cobb County. Maybe you saw that Roy Barnes was quoted in "Around Town" last Wednesday in the Marietta paper. You know Roy Barnes. He's a Methodist, but that's OK. What struck me about what all he said last Wednesday is how he talked about how important it was for him to do what was best, not for his party, but for our county, when he served on the State Senate floor, even though what he was doing was likely to cost him an election:

One of the great things about Cobb County is that even when the Democrats and Republicans were changing from Democrats to Republicans, there was one thing that we had in common. If it affected Cobb County and was good for Cobb County, all of us were going to support it, whether it was Democratic or Republican.

He told about building Barrett Parkway and the East-West Connector. Can you imagine if those weren't there? Rather than take credit for these great road-building projects, which opened up our country to business and new residents, he said, "It was all of us working together." Yet, once Joe Mack Wilson told Barnes, "Now you realize what all this is doing? It's just going to bring in more Republicans." Barnes responded, "Yes, that's probably true, but, Joe, we've got to do it. We're going to do what's best for Cobb

County regardless."

That's it, isn't it?

"If you're going to grow, if you're going to prosper," you've got to do what's best rather than just hold onto what you have, burying it where no one else can benefit from it, for sometimes fighting to maintain what you have is the best way to lose it all.

There were three slaves.

The one who was given five talents took his talents and made five more. The one who was given two talents took his talents and made two more. Then the one who was given one talent took his talent and buried it in the ground.

What do you see here?

Maybe you see two whom you'd like to hire as your wealth advisors. On the other hand, maybe you see that two were willing to take a risk with what wasn't theirs while the third was cautious and conservative, or maybe you see that two acted purely out of love for their master with little concern for whether or not they'd disappoint him, while the third acted completely out of fear.

Has fear ever played such a role in your life?

Sometimes you fear that you might lose what you have, so you hold on too tightly. Sometimes you fear disappointing anyone, but you end up disappointing everyone. Sometimes you fear failure, so you never really try.

That's the culture in some households.

That's how some people were raised.

Their mothers couldn't stand the thought of broken plates or a cavities. I grew up in a house where mistakes were OK and so was breaking things. In fact, if there wasn't a flathead screwdriver handy, my dad would grab a butter knife from the silverware drawer. If we were having guests over and needed more place settings, my mom might send us to the sandbox to collect all the missing spoons. However, not every household is like that.

In some kitchens, children start crying as soon as a glass slips out of their hands because they know that making a mess is just cause for condemnation. The third slave assumed his master was like that, and so he explains:

Master, I knew that you were a harsh man, reaping where you did not sow, and gathering where you did not scatter seed; so I was afraid, and I went and hid your talent in the ground. Here you have what is yours.

What I love is how the master responds:

You knew, did you?

You knew, did you, that I reap where I did not sow, and gather where I did not scatter?

You knew that I'd punish you if you messed up?

You knew that I'm harsh and ungenerous?

Where did you get that idea? From the year's wages that I gave you for no reason?

What we have here in this parable is a failure to communicate because this slave is sure that he knows the master, while being completely and horribly wrong.

Has that ever happened to you?

Have you ever misjudged the master?

I do that all the time.

Let me give you an example.

You might know this, but we have the most incredible food distribution ministry. The School Board recognized our church at their meeting last week. Rev. Cassie Waits and Aimee Bush were there to be recognized and thanked. Aimee has been running a tight ship, organizing a great team of volunteers, and even driving a great, big refrigeration truck that holds our milk and chicken while we give it out. The need is great. Right now, people are driving here from the Six Flags area because there are so few places that are able to distribute food during this pandemic. Every Monday, enough food for 1,500 meals is dropped off at the church from the Atlanta Food Bank. Can you imagine what 1,500 meals worth of spaghetti looks like?

I've told you that we've distributed more than 200,000 lbs. of food, which is hard to quantify. The better visual is a line of cars that fills up our main parking lot and then circles the big parking lot across the tracks. We provide several days' worth to 250 families every Monday. We're talking about hundreds of cars, yet one volunteer, Fran Brailsford, knows all their faces and remembers so many of their names.

I was standing out there with Fran and Andrea Freund. Andrea has to watch traffic so that she can send cars down Kennesaw Avenue from our north parking lot into our main parking lot without stopping the flow of traffic. It's quite aprocess, and it's a lot of cars, so I assumed that when a neighbor who lives right by our church called to talk about the food distribution, he was calling to ask why it was taking him so long to get home from work, and if I could do anything about all these cars backing up traffic.

Why would I assume that?

It's because when people call me, sometimes I assume they're calling me with a problem. When the principle calls you to her office, you don't assume it's to receive a lollipop; likewise, sometimes people call me, and if they say, "Joe, I'd like to talk with you about something," my first impulse is to think it's bad, only when I returned this wonderful man's phone call, he told me that he'd like to donate $7,500 to feed even more people than we are already.

Why do we live in such fear?

Why do we misjudge the Master when the Master has already done so much for us?

In a culture of fear, we must remember Who our Master is and what He intends for us, so I remind you of these words from our first Scripture lesson:

God has destined us not for wrath but for obtaining salvation through our Lord Jesus Christ.

Don't misjudge the Master.

Don't mistake His intention for you.

Don't fail to see His hand at work in your life.

Don't ignore the sound of His voice proclaiming His undying love, for He is our God, and He has destined us not for wrath but salvation.

Amen.

Let the Same Mind Be in You
Ephesians 1: 15-23 and Matthew 25: 31-46
Preached on November 22, 2020

Today is Christ the King Sunday; this is a Sunday that reminds us Who is truly King, to Whom we owe allegiance, Who it is that can lead us to a better place than the one we find ourselves in right now, and what this true King requires of us.

We're all serving somebody, but whom are we serving, and what does he require?

Sara and I have been watching *The Crown* on *Netflix*. Season four is now out. I don't know about you, but when there's anything new to watch on TV, I get terribly excited. Margaret Thatcher shows up in season four, and so does Diana, and it's the ending of their first episode together that I'd now like to ruin for you if you haven't already seen it.

Please forgive me.

Margaret Thatcher, the Prime Minister, shows up to spend some time with the royal family at their castle in Scotland. It's a hard thing to go up and spend some time at anyone's home because you may not know all the rules: what's dinner attire? Should we have brought something? Does everyone come down to breakfast still in his pj's?

Such waters become exponentially more difficult to navigate when you are in the home of the English Royal Family. The Prime Minister and her husband know all that, so they're visibly nervous about meeting the standards of their host, the Queen, as they're shown to their rooms, and they can immediately tell that here the rules are different from what they're accustomed to because, when in Scotland, spouses in the home of the Royal Family don't sleep in the same bed or even stay in the same bedroom.

Fortunately, there is an itinerary for their stay. It's been printed and placed on a table, so they know that the next gathering is that evening, though it's not clear if one should come down to drinks at 6:00 already dressed for dinner, which is black tie. The Thatchers decided to go down prepared for dinner. However, when they come down for drinks at 6:00 in their formal attire, they join the Royal Family, who's just come in from stalking a stag. They're all muddy in their hiking boots and are surprised by what the Thatchers have on. You see, they're already falling short. The next day, the Queen invites the Prime Minister to go out to stalk this stag.

Unfortunately, the Prime Minister only brought her sensible heels, which is the wrong footwear for traversing the Scottish Highlands.

That evening, the Royal Family plays parlor games.

Margaret Thatcher doesn't play parlor games.

Basically, it's all a failure for the Thatchers. The Prime Minister is judged harshly, and she goes home early, defeated. Then the young woman who would be Princess Diana shows up.

She makes everyone laugh.

She spots the stag they've been stalking.

She wins at parlor games, and it's clear that she's done what she needed to have done to gain the approval of the Royal Family, only, at the end of the episode, as the paparazzi learns that Diana is the Prince's new love interest, they begin to surround her with their flashing cameras as servants back in Scotland are hanging the mounted stag's head on the wall, and it becomes clear that while Diana has been accepted, her acceptance comes at a cost.

We all bow before somebody, but whose acceptance are we working for?

Princess Diana had the perfect wedding by royal standards. Do you remember how long the train was on her gown that nearly filled up Westminster Abby? She met their expectations, she rose to the occasion, but she walked down the aisle and married a man who loved another woman. Sometimes, we serve masters who seem to offer salvation, so we grovel before them and rise to their expectations, yet what do they really give?

Today is Christ the King Sunday: a Sunday that reminds us Who is truly King and Who can lead us to a better place than the one we find ourselves in right now.

Considering where we are right now, I wonder if life feels to you anything like it must have felt to Moses and the Israelites, standing on the beach, with the Egyptian army closing in. There's nowhere to go, as we can't just march through the sea. Life isn't normal, but neither has the road back to normal been made clear. God will save us, but we must wait, and we must not turn on each other while we wait or there won't be anything left for Him to save.

Hear what he requires of those whom He'll lead across the sea and into the Promised Land: *Come, you that are blessed by my Father, inherit the kingdom prepared for you from the foundation of the world; for I was hungry and you gave me food, I was thirsty and you gave me something to drink, I was a stranger and you welcomed me, I was naked and you gave me clothing, I was sick and you took care of me, I was in prison and you visited me.*

His point is that how we treat each other, maybe especially in a climate where nothing goes exactly as it should, matters most. Yet, some make rising to the same standards of perfection set by human society, which were unattainable before all this started, their chief priority, prompting the question: whom do we really serve?

Our wedding wasn't like Diana's.

I've been thinking about our wedding because last Monday was our 18th wedding anniversary. The ceremony was supposed to be outside, but it rained.

I was given this one job: find someone who can sing, and I did, only I'd never asked to hear him sing, and while he did sing, he shouldn't have.

There was a band, but they spent all their time eating rather than playing, and they didn't know the words to the song we wanted them to play for our first dance, so we used a CD, only the CD skipped.

In so many ways, we failed to rise to the standards in our minds. Certainly, this was no Royal Wedding, but we love each other. We still do, and it is by the standard of how well we all love each other that we will be judged by the King of Kings. Not everyone seems to know that, but notice how He just comes right out and says it, "I'm King of Kings, and if you want Me to welcome you into My kingdom, pay attention to the least of these. Wear sensible high heels all you want, just pay attention to the poor."

Is He the One Whose acceptance we are working for?

In our world today, it's getting even harder to follow the social protocol because it's not university accepted what we should be doing.

It reminds me of that wonderful line about the chaos of the time of Judges: "In those days there was no king in Israel; all people did what was right in their own eyes." Likewise, some wear masks, and some don't. You'll be judged by someone either way.

Our world is so full of judgement.

An old preacher used to say that far too many churchgoers have grown used to having Kentucky Fried Pastor for lunch after worship. They gather around the table to debate how long or how short the sermon was. The congregation judges the preacher, the preacher judges the congregation, husbands judge their wives, wives judge their husbands, sisters judge each other, and sometimes we judge just to have something to talk about with friends.

We even judge ourselves.

We don't just look in the mirror. No, we look in the mirror, and we compare ourselves to some standard. Do I look young enough? Do I look trim enough? Am I pretty enough? Every student in high school does the same thing. She thinks about what she'll wear and how she'll act because she knows she's being judged and watched, not just graded by her teachers but also assessed as worthy or unworthy based on her looks.

I'd like to say that at some point it gets easier.

It does, but it also never ends until we settle on whose acceptance we're willing to work for.

Let it be the One Who will have final judgement over you.

Consider not what this world wants from you, but what He requires:

I was hungry and you gave me food, I was thirsty and you gave me something to drink, I was a stranger and you welcomed me, I was naked and you gave me clothing, I was sick and you took care of me, I was in prison and you visited me.

That's what finally matters.

That's how you'll make perfect memories.

That's what really fulfills us and makes us people we're proud to be.

How do you treat people?

Our wedding was perfect because the woman I'm married to is whom I love.

I don't always wear the right clothes, or do the right things, but ultimately, I'll not be judged by my clothes or my deeds; I'll be judged by the standards set by the God of love.

Let the same mind be in you that was in the Christ Jesus,

Who, though he was in the form of God,

Did not regard equality with God as something to be exploited,

But emptied himself, taking the form of a slave, being born in human likeness.

And being found in human form, he humbled himself

And became obedient to the point of death – even death on a cross.

We are all standing on the shore, and the only way to get to the Promised Land is for God to deliver us, though what we do now matters. We only have the power to treat each other well, and by our love, they'll know we are Christians.

Amen.

They Came Confessing Their Sins
Isaiah 11: 1-9 and Mark 1: 1-8
Preached on December 6, 2020

Every year at about this time, we turn our attention to John the Baptist, and this year, what amazes me about John the Baptist are the crowds. According to our second Scripture lesson from the Gospel of Mark, the city and the countryside emptied out and lined up to be in his presence, which this time of year, sounds something like the kind of audience only the likes of Santa Clause would be able to command. Notice, then, how it's not lines of parents with children who are lining up to see him. Lining up to see John the Baptist are grown men and women.

I believe that's an important detail to pay attention to because, in our culture, what adults are willing to go out of their way to do often seems to have a lot more to do with what their kids want or need than what they themselves want or need.

For example, I don't know many adults who frequent McDonald's for their own benefit.

In fact, if I were given the choice, I'd rather eat about anything than a chicken nugget shaped like a cowboy boot. However, if I had a granddaughter who wanted a happy meal, I'd gladly suffer through. Maybe that's just how it is. Something that may be true about our culture is that we will just do all kinds of things to make kids happy, and so, maybe you, like me, are wondering who in their right mind would travel out into the desert to confess?

Who even has time in his schedule for that?

Yet, they swarmed him.

They made it a priority to go and see him it seems, even though he was way out there.

I don't know how far they all had to travel. Surely, it wasn't on a paved road. They likely had to diverge from the paths of their daily routines to walk through the sand and scrub of the wilderness to get to the river, which is something that I know people are willing to do, but not often for themselves.

Think about what we'll do for our kids.

I showed up outside the Marietta Center for Advanced Academics at 4 AM to make sure that our daughter got in. It was raining, and the man at the front of the line was in his camo coveralls. He had one of those pop-up tents and one of those nice folding chairs that reclines. When they opened the doors, he had fallen asleep, and we all just walked right passed him.

I said to the guy next to me, "Shouldn't we wake him up?" It turns out, someone else was looking out for him. His kid got in, too, but my point is that we'll do almost anything for our kids, while the grown-ups in our second Scripture lesson didn't go out into the desert on behalf of their children's education.

When I was a kid in little league, my parents paid for me to have a private batting instructor. Imagine that. I was so well cared for. My dad would come home from work having already sat in traffic, then he'd get right back in it to drive me out to this special lesson. On the other hand, those crowds didn't go out into the desert to see John so that their kids would have a leg up on the baseball field.

They went for themselves.

These people went out to the river Jordan to see John, who was clothed with camel's hair, with a leather belt around his waist. It wasn't for their kids. It was for them to confess.

We need to think about that.

Especially these days, we need to think about what we will travel long distances for and for whom we will make sacrifices because so many among us will go through hardship and will take risk to make sure that the kids they love have the chance to stand before a certain man with a long beard wearing a strange outfit; yet, it's not John the Baptist, and it's not for them. As a culture, we don't have any problem teaching our kids that it's OK to want something for Christmas, but what do you want?

What do I want?

I remember how long the lines were when I was a kid.

We'd first have a special breakfast, then we'd ride the Pink Pig, before standing in the longest line to sit on Santa's lap, laying before him all our Christmas wishes. This year, many will still go see him because it's important. It's not wrong to be able to say what it is that you want. That's a skill kids need to have.

It's OK to want things, so we encourage our kids to write it all down.

Even if they can only just slip their lists into a slot rather than place them in Santa's hand. Did you hear that pandemic Santa smiles from within this sanitary snow globe-like enclosure so no germs are exchanged?

Things are different this year.

Still, we want to make sure that our kids can make their wishes known.

Our girls have made their lists. Lily turned hers into a power point presentation, with music. I'm serious. The slides have different color backgrounds: purple if she really wants it, blue if she just sort of does. There's a picture of the item on each slide, a link for her grandparents to click on, which makes buying for her very convenient, and I've been there encouraging her through each draft of this presentation that she started back in October because I want our daughters to be able to stand up and tell the world what they want.

I want them to be honest and clear about what they need.

On the other hand, we don't really encourage adults to do that sort of thing.

"What do you want to have for dinner?" a husband asked his wife.

"I don't care," she responded.

It's hard for some adults to put stuff on a Christmas list because they're used to paying attention to what other people want and need, and maybe we shouldn't be spending time on Christmas lists, yet all those grown-ups went out of their way to see John the Baptist.

Why?

What does he have to offer?

Some kids have their lists all typed up:

- Nintendo switch

- Baby Alive

- Hot Wheels Ultimate Garage

What about their parents?

Some dad will ask for a nice bottle of scotch, only what will really give him some real, true peace? I can image a mother who can't think of anything to ask for, so her kids will probably just get her another scarf. Who needs another scarf?

What if instead, she doesn't think about Santa this year and instead imagines herself lining up to see John. What if we were all to imagine ourselves lining up at the river to ask for the number one thing that every mother and father really wants and needs?

I don't even remember where I heard this. It might not be based on a study or any real data; still, it rings true: what every father wants more than anything else is just to be appreciated by his family, and what every mother so truly wants is to be forgiven.

Does that sound right?

There's a comedian who has this bit about how no one ever gives dad credit for anything. Polite sons know to thank their mothers for dinners made and stuff like that, but none of them ever say, "Hey, Dad, I sure to appreciate how you worked so hard to keep on the lights in this house. I just want to thank you for paying the mortgage, Dad."

Can you imagine that?

Dads want to be appreciated.

That's maybe what's on their Christmas lists.

Could that be true?

That way of thinking is based on a generalization: one that's not always true for most families, as so many women are now the bread winners, but maybe it sounds close enough and maybe this does, too: that so many mothers live with the fear of what their children are telling their therapists about them.

If any of this regarding mothers and fathers really just wanting appreciation and forgiveness rings true, then think about John the Baptist as some kind of Santa Clause for grown-ups because instead of a wish list of presents, people voice to him all their mistakes, regrets, and second guessing. Then, on Christmas morning, they look under the tree to find God's grace. That's nice to think about, isn't it?

Yet, that's what this is all about.

John called people to be honest about the desires of their hearts, so what heavy burden do you want to lay down?

What mistake did you make that you need to be forgiven for?

What did you say that you wish you never would have said?

What did you do that you wish you never would have done?

Speak now and know that One is coming Who has healing in His wings.

What we see here in the Gospel of Mark is just the tip of the iceberg of the great miracle of Christianity, the true center of our faith: the real focal point, the chief creed, the unique and defining attribute of what is required to follow Jesus, namely, opening ourselves up to receive the grace He brings.

My world religions teacher said it like that in college. Someone asked him, "what is unique about Christianity?" There are so many commonalities between the great world religions, what makes Christianity different? He said it was grace; that in all the world's great religions, all those faiths that call people to higher ideals of love and hope, it is Christianity that most boldly proclaims among them all that your imperfection is no hinderance.

You don't need to be ashamed or afraid.

Be honest before God about what you wished you'd done and just start again.

It's not too late.

Today is a new day.

That feels to me like an especially important message this year because who among us really feels like right now, this year, that he is being his best self? You know what our girls told me? They said, "Daddy, you've gotten a lot meaner since you turned 40." I don't think that's true, but things do grate on me more now than they used to.

I am shorter with them than I want to be. Being on *Zoom* calls for hours at a time is just doing something to my head, so when they leave their lunch boxes on the floor in the kitchen or yell at each other in the living room, it pushes me over the edge a lot sooner than it did a year ago. Maybe we're all stretched a little too thin.

Maybe we're wearing down in ways we're not used to.

Let me tell you this, too: that world religions professor from college, I walked into his classroom on the day of the test, only I didn't know it was the day of the test. He could tell I was surprised and unprepared, and so he offered me grace. He said, "You can come to my office in two days to take the test then." Well, I did that, only I wasn't prepared two days later either. Why? Because grace without repentance is wasted grace. Admitting that there's something not quite right is the perfect place for our grown-up Christmas lists to start. Why? Because Grace is coming, but to receive it, we must first get OK with the truth that we all need it.

Amen.

What Child Is This?
Ezra 3: 10-13 and Luke 1: 46-55
Preached on December 13, 2020

Some years ago, I was a camp counselor at Camp Cherokee, which was a church camp the churches in our Presbytery organized on Lake Allatoona. My sister, Elizabeth, and I grew up going there. When we were old enough, we both became counselors. Every week of camp, there'd be a different preacher who would lead the evening worship service for all the young campers, and one of their sermons comes to mind in thinking about this passage of Scripture, where Mary reacts to the news that she will be the mother of our Savior.

This preacher didn't beat around the bush.

He had something he wanted to say, and he was going to say it whether it was appropriate for young ears to hear or not. He was really focused on the Lord's crucifixion. "Did you know, children," he says, "that after the Lord was betrayed, He was arrested, but the Roman soldiers weren't kind to our Lord. No, they whipped Him. They whipped and whipped Him within an inch of His life, but it wasn't quite enough to kill Him."

"After they whipped Him, they put this awful crown of thorns on His head so that blood dripped down His face, but children, it wasn't the crown of thorns that killed Him either. Since He was still within an inch of His life, they took these old, rusty nails. They took these big, rusty nails, and they nailed Him through the arm and to this wooden cross, only it wasn't the rusty nails that killed Him either. Do you know what finally killed Him, children?"

And I could hear it from the back of the group: just a whisper from a boy of eight or nine: "Was it tetanus?"

I love that story.

The preacher is trying to make one point, only a young boy speaks up to make another, and in that moment, one sermon gave way to an experience that brings me joy every time I think of it.

Surprise is one place joy comes from, isn't it?

This Sunday of the season of Advent, we light the third Advent candle, the Candle of Joy. It's particularly appropriate that the Foster family light the Joy

Candle because that was Natalie Foster's mother's name, so today we celebrate joy, but think with me about where joy comes from.

Don't we so often find joy in the unexpected?

Don't you see joy when the daily grind blooms in surprises?

That's how it is sometimes. Sometimes, when everything goes according to plan, life becomes boring and monotonous, and sometimes, when everything goes wrong, it goes exactly right. Sometimes, the best laid schemes of mice and men fall apart, and what gives way are stories truly worth telling and remembering.

The best Christmas movies are like that.

Think about *Home Alone*. In the movie *Home Alone*, in one sense, everything goes absolutely wrong. What could be worse than forgetting your child at home when flying to Paris? That's what happens in the movie, though. Kevin, who was no older than the little camper in my story, gets left all alone at Christmas. At first, it's an exciting adventure for him. For his mother, it was her worst nightmare, but what starts off in a nightmare turns into little Kevin learning to value his family. A lesson is learned because they forgot him and left him at home all by himself. Now that wasn't a well- executed family trip, yet something so good came out of it.

In the same way, think about *How the Grinch Stole Christmas*. No one hopes to have her tree stolen by a broken-hearted man covered in green fur, but when the Whos down in Whoville find that everything is gone on Christmas morning, what do they do? They sing.

Then there's our family favorite, *National Lampoon's Christmas Vacation*. We watched it last weekend, and our daughters couldn't believe how their parents laughed at all these jokes they considered to be highly inappropriate, yet it is hilarious. It's hilarious how Clark Griswold works and works and works to enhance everyone's Christmas cheer, yet nothing goes right. The turkey is dry, one lady wraps up her cat as a present, Snot the dog gags on a bone from under the table, and Cousin Eddie empties the you-know-what in the storm drain, for despite all our hard work, it appears as though all we're going to get some years is a subscription to the Jelly of the Month Club or worse.

This has been a challenging year.

In some ways, this has been a nightmare of a year.

Have you seen the 2020-themed Christmas ornaments? We have special, commemorative ornaments on our tree that represent different milestones. The 2002 ornament from Sara's mom has wedding bells on it because that was our first Christmas together as husband and wife. Sara's mom also gave us new baby ornaments for 2009 and 2011 for our daughters' first Christmases, but have you seen the 2020 commemorative ornaments?

One has Santa with an N-95 mask on.

Another is a garbage dumpster on fire.

I just designed one for the Fosters because little Harry, their four-year-old, got his head stuck in the banisters of their staircase. Jon made the mistake of sending me a picture, which I've sent off to a company to turn into a glass ornament, so they'll always remember just what this crazy year was like. The Grinch would say that this year stink, stank, stunk, but if we look to Mary, then comes the reminder that among our shattered expectations is the promise of God.

We know her song well.

It's been sung and sung, again and again.

We call it the Magnificat, a beautiful title rooted in the word *magnificence*; yet consider the context in which she sang that song. She had just been told by an angel that she would become the mother to our Savior. That's good news, only what child is this?

Being pregnant wasn't part of her plan.

She wasn't even married.

Do you think she grew up dreaming of the year she'd become an unwed teenage mother?

Do you think she was hoping to be the subject of whisper and rumor, a stress on her poor mother and a shame on her father?

That Christmas so long ago, was anything going according to how she envisioned it? No, but consider how when all her plans go up in smoke, she sings because Mary sees something larger than life unfolding before her. She feels a promise growing in her womb. She knew that in her life, a dream was becoming a reality, a bright future that she could not have imagined, only for it to be realized, she must accept that Christmas can no longer be about her plans.

What we see in her song is that faithful Mary knows that this is about God's plans, so rather than sing a sad lamentation as everything she wrote down in her wedding book planner is going up in flames, Mary rejoices, for she knows that sometimes God makes a mockery of our best laid plans to give a gift that's even better.

That's what happens in all the best Christmas movies.

Do you remember how Cousin Eddie kidnaps Clark's boss and brings him back hogtied in his bathrobe? Now the Griswolds are truly in the midst of a disaster. Clark has basically already ruined everything in his attempt to hold it all together, only it's about to get worse, because the SWAT team is poised to capture the kidnapper, and Clark can see himself spending the rest of Christmas in jail.

Think about what all is going on here.

Things are now very bad, when suddenly the boss can see that not giving his employees their Christmas bonuses was the wrong move. Everything is falling apart, while somehow, in the midst of the chaos, he is busy recognizing what really matters. Clark's boss is facing the uncomfortable truth about himself and wrestling with what he should have done all along but didn't and what he can do next to somehow make it all right.

That's what he sees as his world is turned upside down.

He's seeing things while at the mercy of a kindhearted doofus, only through his unexpected Christmas Eve, this powerful corporate mogul discovers what Christmas really is.

The mess has to happen, for the proud must change and be reborn.

That's another reason we love Mary's song.

We love to hear it because it's beautiful, only it's not holly-jolly, radio-ready, Christmas fluff. It's justice, righteousness, and joy springing from ashes.

My soul magnifies the Lord, and my spirit rejoices in God my Savior,

His mercy is for those who fear him from generation to generation.

He has shown strength with his arm;

He has scattered the proud in the thoughts of their hearts.

He has brought down the powerful from their thrones,

Are you ready for that?

Are your eyes open to that?

They may as well be because we're right in the middle of it.

This year, we can't gather for Christmas Eve services as we always have. I'm the most disappointed that we can't have our family service, but that doesn't mean families aren't gathering here. In fact, 350 families are lining up in our parking lot every Monday to receive boxes from the Atlanta Food Bank containing five complete meals each.

For some reason, the Atlanta Food Bank gave us boxes and boxes of garlic lastweek. Thank goodness no one brought all those boxes inside, or we'd still be smelling it, but that's hardly the point. The point is that there is such a profound need in our community, and had we all been rushing around like always, I don't know if I would have seen it. This year was different. This year, the unemployed and underemployed are impossible for me to ignore because they are in our parking lot.

My eyes are open, though my plans are falling apart.

We want Christmas to be perfect, while this year it's being interrupted.

Some of us will have to adapt to new ways of doing things.

Some of us will be by ourselves this Christmas, which I hate, but consider this: every year, some people are alone on Christmas, we just don't always think about it. Now that you're thinking about them, hear the invitation to really see them.

That's what Christmas really is.

In *Home Alone*, it took having a nightmare Christmas to discover the miracle of family that they had been taking for granted. In *How the Grinch Stole Christmas*, it took stealing Christmas for him to understand. In *Christmas Vacation*, Clark's plans must go up in flames for him to erupt in joy as his boss's hardened heart changed, finally seeing his employees as people.

This year, we all have to think about Christmas differently. Inspired by Mary's song, we faithful people must imagine how that can be a blessing. We sing, "What child is this?" and the answer is, He is the One Who changes things.

Take this year of change as an opportunity to value what you've taken for granted, to celebrate what's become tired routine, and to find joy in the unexpected.

May Christ's peace rise from the ashes of your best laid plans, for He is coming, and He comes to make all things new.

Amen.

Surprised by a Fulfilled Prophecy
Jeremiah 31: 31-34 and Luke 1: 67-80
Preached on December 20, 2020

We're now getting very close to the big day, the most important day for most every child in every state of our nation. The morning when, having made their lists and been as good as possible, they drag their sleeping parents out of bed and rush to the living room to see what Santa's left under the Christmas Tree.

It's a morning of promises fulfilled.

Of wishes made and granted.

Christmas morning is the essence of hope and joy.

Even if there's not peace on earth exactly or abundant blessing on all humankind on Christmas morning, it feels like it for just a minute. It's fleeting, but it's there. Even if before the wrapping paper is even cleaned up, most of our kids will be thinking about what they'd like to get next year, there is something beautiful about their attitude.

Yet, think about it.

Regardless of the self-interest and materialism, they're kids who know that dreams do come true, and if you really want something, you might just get it. Adults don't think about it that way. On Christmas morning, we stand back and watch it happen without feeling exactly the same hopefulness and joy ourselves.

Of course, adults still love Christmas morning.

I love Christmas morning, but I don't look at it the same way I once did. I don't look forward to it as our girls are looking forward to it right now. I wonder if many adults, like me, would rather have Santa come down the chimney to pack up some stuff from my basement and take it back to the North Pole than have him deliver anything else.

A member of our church had too much, so she was having a yard sale last weekend. She's someone with outstanding taste, so as soon as Sara and I heard about it, we made our way to her driveway. Then, last Sunday, when a nice armchair hadn't sold, she invited us back over to pick it up if we still wanted it. Well, we did, and while I was loading it into our car, I asked her what the yard sale had been like. Most people don't like yard sales. I don't like the hassle of hauling everything outside, then getting up early to stand around while people pick over my stuff. Interestingly, this woman said that the hard part of having a yard sale for her was giving up and moving on.

"To have a yard sale, you're admitting that you're not going to get to all those things you thought you would. If you're selling it, then you're facing the fact that you're never really going to learn how to re-cane those chairs or refinish that dresser." Your son is never going to come back for his catcher's mitt. Your daughter really doesn't want her grandmother's paintings. To have a yard sale, you have to give up on something you imagined or promised yourself that you would do, which is even harder than finding out that some people are only willing to pay fifty cents for what you paid $50 for.

Most children aren't ever thinking like that this time of year or any time of year.

They're still filling up their lives, not downsizing.

To them, the whole world is full of possibility, and their dreams are coming true on Christmas morning.

They're good at wishing for something.

On the other hand, some of their parents have had to master the art of letting go, moving on, and settling for less. If we didn't, imagine how full all our basements would be.

A bride hangs onto her wedding dress, imagining that one day her daughter will wear it.

A groom hangs onto his tuxedo, imaging that he'll fit into it again.

It's a hard thing to face the fact that neither of those things are likely to happen, so congratulate yourself if you've had a yard sale. Give someone else the chance to make his own pasta or brew her own beer, but be careful.

Let go of your motorcycle, but don't let go of adventure.

Let go of your golf clubs, but find another way of getting outside.

Let go of your bassinette, but don't give up on the future; don't give up on the promise.

For Zechariah, it had been so long, surely he had given up on the idea that it would ever happen. Our second Scripture lesson from Luke is the account of what Zechariah said once he had finally regained his speech. What he says in our second Scripture lesson is in celebration of his son John the Baptist's birth, but the background for this Scripture lesson is that he had been waiting for a child so long that the bassinette had been sold or given away.

They wanted a child, but the child never came, so rather than keep wishing, they let go.

Is that wrong?

Well, it depends.

Elizabeth and Zechariah were good and righteous people. The Gospel of Luke goes so far as to say that they were, "Both of them... righteous before God, living blamelessly according to all the commandments and regulations of the Lord." Not only that, Zechariah was a priest, and Elizabeth was a descendant of Aaron, the original priest of Israel, yet none of that guarantees their lives are full of faith, hope, and love.

None of that ensures that they really expected the living God to step into their lives.

What we should all assume is that they knew how to pray, while at some point they started to wonder, "What's the point?"

Month by month, the disappointment became too much to take, and rather than be the victims of their high expectations, they lowered their sights and settled into the reality that children would just not be in the cards. After all, "both were getting on in years," and part of growing up is letting go of fairy tale dreams, so they had a yard sale and let go.

Zechariah continued on as a priest.

He kept wearing his priestly garments, saying his priestly prayers, and was surely honored when he was chosen to go offer incense in the holiest place on earth, the sanctuary of the temple, the place where all good Jews knew God was most truly present.

Surely, he was honored, but as a man who had gotten good at letting go of some of his dreams and some of his hopes, did he still believe he might meet God there?

Had it been you, what would you have expected?

Parents know that their kids are growing up when they stop believing in certain things, only where does the stop-believing-in stop? If your kids like *Harry Potter*, maybe you broke the news that an acceptance letter from Hogwarts School of Witchcraft and Wizardry isn't coming. Still, don't you want them to believe that the world is full of magic?

At some point, I had to let go of my dreams of being a professional baseball player, but did I also let go of the idea that I could be anything I dreamed I could be?

Zechariah had stopped asking his wife Elizabeth about it.

Now a stomach bug was always just a stomach bug.

Having given up on that dream, as he entered the Temple, the place thought to be the sanctuary of God, did he expect anything special to happen?

What did he expect to see?

When we start letting go, it's so easy to let go of too much.

The words we say in here can become empty so that it's easy to participate in the rituals without believing that they mean much of anything.

How often have I said to you, "Know that you are forgiven, and be at peace," and how often have you really believed it?

How often have I stood at the table, reminding you that Christ died for your salvation, and how often have you really taken it in?

I think this is true of Zechariah, that this man who must have known all the stories of Scripture by heart, all the accounts of God speaking to Abraham and Sarah and Rahab and Jacob and Moses, all the times angels appeared, all the miraculous events that changed the course of history. Still, this man was terrified when an angel of the Lord was there, exactly in the place that an angel of the Lord is supposed to be because he had let go of too much. He had even let go of the truth that God is alive and makes miracles happen.

We are now very close to the big day.

Christmas.

And Christmas is about this God being born.

Christmas is about God really being born and walking around on the earth, only do you really believe He's coming? Are you really ready for His birth, or have you given up believing such miraculous things?

Zechariah wasn't a faithless person. He was a priest after all, but when an angel really showed up and told him that his prayer for a child would be answered, he was terrified. His wife, on the other hand, was faithful, and Luke tells us that she said, "This is what the Lord has done for me when the Lord looked favorably on me and took away the disgrace I have endured among my people." Yet because of his faithlessness, the angel made Zechariah mute. Finally, once he was able to speak again, having only been able to watch and listen, he spoke the second Scripture lesson, which we just read, not like a rational, measured old man, having learned how to give up on his unfulfilled dreams, but like a faithful prophet, having had his eyes opened to the God Who is still at work in this world doing impossible things.

There is so much ritual to our celebration of Christmas. Do not forget that there is something wonderfully real beneath all the wrapping paper. Behind and under every tradition is a love that changes everything.

By the tender mercy of our God,

The dawn from on high will break upon us,

To give light to those who sit in darkness and in the shadow of death,

To guide our feet into the way of peace.

These are not empty words. This is no idle tale. This is the prophecy fulfilled. The Good News of our Lord Jesus Christ.

Amen.

Christmas and a New Year

Even when it's a day with four worship services, the last of which ends at midnight, Christmas Eve is my favorite day of the year. This year was my first Christmas Eve as a pastor where I was only a part of one service. With much less to do on Christmas Eve, I was surprised by how disappointed I was. I missed the busyness of it. Also, the empty Great Hall where the worship service was recorded was so different from the packed Christmas Eve crowd that I'm used to.

Regardless, Christmas Eve is still my favorite day of the year, for it is the night we celebrate the birth of hope. As Christmas Eve gave way to a new year, and the hoped-for vaccine became a reality, in the season the following sermons were preached, there was so much to celebrate and give thanks to God for.

However, this hope stood in stark contrast to certain realities.

While many in the United States looked forward to the vaccine, other nations of the world still had a long time to wait. In January, Washington, D.C. was stormed by those who questioned the election's legitimacy. There was controversy over the vaccine and controversy over the election. It was a strange time and an important time to holdtight to hope.

Fear Not

Isaiah 9: 2-7 and Luke 2: 1-20

Preached on December 24, 2020

The Scripture lesson I just read from the Gospel of Luke is the same one read by Linus in *A Charlie Brown Christmas*. It's a well-known passage, featuring those mainstays of every nativity scene: the shepherds, who answered the call from the angels to go and see this thing that God had done on that very first Christmas so long ago.

I wonder if they left their flocks behind or brought them.

Does that sound like a good question?

It might sound too fanciful or beside the point, as our questions often are.

In the comics last Sunday, the mom in "The Family Circus" was trying to tell the Christmas story but couldn't for all the kids who were asking:

Who wrote this story?

Should Joseph have called sooner to get a reservation at the Inn?

Why didn't the Wise Men bring baby Jesus some better presents?

I don't mean to get in the way of the story with this question, but truly, I do think about the flocks, and I bet they left them because hearing the great Good News that changes everything demands that we leave something behind, namely, our fear. To quote from the 90s movie *Defending Your Life*, "Fear is like a giant fog. It sits on your brain and blocks everything – real feelings, true happiness, real joy. They can't get through that fog. But you lift it, and buddy, you're in for the ride of your life."

That's how it was.

Maybe they left one shepherd behind the way Neil Armstrong and Buzz Aldrin walked on the moon while what's-his-name stayed back on the ship. We remember the shepherds because they took that step of faith right over their fear. That's worth thinking about on Christmas Eve. In this season of abundant anxiety, "Fear not," is the part of this second Scripture lesson that I find impossible to ignore because that's just such a challenge in the time of a viral pandemic.

"Fear not," is a radical instruction in this time when there is much to fear.

Yet, something that I never would have noticed on my own is that as Linus, the "Peanuts" character known for always carrying around his blankie, drops it when he says this verse from the Gospel of Luke, "And the angel said unto them, 'Fear not!'"

There's a message for this age that glimmers from that scene as well as from all the best Christmas movies.

"Fear not," George Bailey. "And see that you've had a wonderful life."

"Fear not," Ebenezer Scrooge. "Your life isn't over. You can do it all differently, starting now." "Fear not," ancient shepherds.

"Fear not," my brothers and sisters, for fear is holding all of us captive in one way or another, and I'm not talking about whether or not you're wearing a mask in public. I'm talking about giving life a chance to be new and surprising. I'm talking about real risk, truly opening yourself up to the transforming power of the Gospel, which requires us to let go of our fear.

My brother-in-law is a Methodist pastor. He's a chaplain down at Oxford College of Emory University, and he frequently writes for the local paper. This week, he pointed out that even Christmas movies like *Home Alone* contain a glimmer of what it means to let go of fear. Do you remember the character with the shovel in that movie: that old man who lurks in the neighborhood salting the sidewalks? The kids in the neighborhood are afraid of him. They call him Old Man Marley, and the rumor is that he distributes the remains of his murder victims in that salt, slowly getting rid of the evidence, bit by bit and piece by piece. On Christmas Eve, he sits down with Kevin, the main character, in church. There it's revealed that Old Man Marley carries guilt more than evil intentions around with him as he salts the sidewalk, having years ago broken ties with his son.

"Why don't you call him?" Kevin asks.

"What if he won't talk to me?" Old Man Marley responds.

You see, he's afraid. There's always something to be afraid of, and this has been a fear-packed year where there's something to be afraid of around each and every corner. The obvious fear is of a virus. Some say it's no worse than the flu, yet it's taken the lives of more than 300,000 Americans. Some compare the daily death count to other tragedies, saying it's like a 9/11 every day. We know it's overwhelming some of our hospitals, it's beating down the work force, making educators do backflips (as though their jobs weren't hard enough already), all while some voices are saying: what's the big deal? It's easy to be afraid of the truth, but it's also easy to be even more afraid when it's not clear what the truth is.

That's made calling home more difficult.

Maybe your mother is relieved that you're not coming. Maybe she's mad and eating at a buffet right now before she goes to Walmart without a mask on. Ours is a Christmas veiled in a fear that not everyone is facing, but all of us are feeling, yet the angels come again with that same message, "Be not afraid, fear not, come to Bethlehem and see." Drop your burden, let go of whatever it is that you've been depending on for comfort, be it denial or hand sanitizer, and take comfort in the truth that God is doing something new tonight that changes things, even though sometimes it's hard to believe that anything could ever really change.

The vaccine is here, but that has some just cautiously optimistic.

For example, my Mom works in mental health at the hospital on a Cherokee reservation, so she's one on that front line to receive a vaccine for this virus, only one of her friends who is Cherokee said, "I was honored that Native Americans are among the first to receive the vaccine, until I started thinking about the last time the government offered to help us out. Is this a cure or another delivery of smallpox blankets?"

It's hard sometimes to get excited about the future if you've been hurt in the past.

It's hard to be hopeful if you've been let down before.

It's hard not to be afraid if you have a good reason to be, but I heard a three-year-old named Dalton quoted this week. She said, "Sometimes it makes me a little nervous to go down the slide," but guess what, she still goes down them, and if we can drop our fear, we're in for the ride of our lives.

That's what the shepherds did.

All at once, they could see that there was a power greater than whatever they were afraid of breaking into the world, and the same is true for us.

That's what Christmas is always all about: God breaking into our lives, revealing what fear has hidden from our eyes.

Think about it.

On Christmas Eve, do you really know enough to be hopeless?

Wayne Dyer, an author, once wrote: "No one really knows enough to be pessimistic," especially on the night before hope was born.

Fear not.

Fear not.

What are you holding so tightly to that you can't hear the angels?

Are you ready to recognize that fear could have you seeing it all wrong?

George Bailey was certain he was a failure. Though he had been a hero his whole life, regret was blinding him to the truth. He's on that bridge, trapped in this whirlwind of emotions and unfulfilled dreams. He never got to do any of the things that he wanted to do. He wanted to travel the world but had to stay home to take care of his family. He wanted to be a war hero, but the brother, whose life he saved, got to do that instead. He saved countless lives, he prevented financial ruin, he elevated the lowly, he prevented the degradation of women, he built a community for families where instead there would be a graveyard, and he looks down into the water from a bridge wondering if it had made a lick of difference.

"Fear not," George Bailey.

"Fear not," Ebenezer. It's not too late. This Christmas Eve, fear not. Let go of such worries. Forget how to keep score. Look up from the water of hopelessness to see the bright shining star overhead, for the angels are singing, "Fear not."

"Fear not," all you nurses, underwater, caring for too many people at once. Rushing from one bedside to the next, while friends go to parties and act like everything is fine. Tonight, fear not because your life of virtue makes a bigger difference than you'll ever know.

"Fear not," all you teachers. Abraham Lincoln had to learn remotely, too, and look at where he ended up.

"Fear not," all you parents, for learning how to do without never hurt anybody, and it won't hurt your kids.

They should fear not as well.

"Fear not," all you children. Tomorrow is a new day, shining bright with potential.

"Fear not," even you who mourn because the God Who takes death's sting away is born unto us. "Fear not" if you're hopeless, for there is more to the story.

Lastly, "Fear not," all you who are alone because you're not. The Light of the World is breaking into our lives. Drop your fear, anxiety, worry, and angst for just long enough to see that something different is happening, for unto us is born this day in the City of David, a Savior, Who is the Messiah, the Lord.

Amen.

Home By Another Road
Matthew 2: 1-12

Preached on January 3, 2021

A couple weeks ago, Keli Gambrill, who is a member of our church and one of our county commissioners, called to ask me if I'd be willing to put together a short article for her weekly newsletter. She's launching a new section of her newsletter asking members of different churches and other organizations in our county the same question, in the hopes that our answers will reveal that we have more in common than we realized, so Commissioner Gambrill and I decided to ask several members of our church, "How has 2020 made you a better person?" Members of our congregation answered this way:

- Wow, I can think of a lot to say about 2020, but can I say it has made me a better person? I'm not sure. Maybe a stronger person? Together, we have all endured a devastating pandemic and a very divisive election. It has been hard not to fall into depression!

-As our social activities narrowed, we spent more time with family.

-We now have closer relationships with our grandchildren. That time was exhausting but precious. It forced me to slow down and relearn patience.

-This spring was especially beautiful, so we spent more time outdoors.

-With so many neighbors working and learning from home, everyone was out walking and biking. I met many neighbors and participated in events to assist local restaurants, food trucks, etc. Relearning the importance of community was a definite positive.

-I can't say for sure I am a better person, but I think I have become a better friend and family member this year. We lost my dad and a friend battled cancer (successfully so far!) and, even though those are difficult walks, I feel relationships got stronger. I worked on not worrying about what I can't change and letting it go to God. Despite this year's losses and disappointments, as it comes to a close, I am hopeful.

-2020 has made me a better person as I have found myself really taking time to learn about myself because I am now alone, sometimes not seeing anyone in person for days. As an extrovert, I have spent time with friends and family on the phone really talking about our lives.

-I am more compassionate than ever before. My heart aches as I try to relate to the suffering that is all around us this year. I have been more giving than before. I also have grown to cherish the importance of family and will never again take the time spent together for granted.

What I hear in those responses is that something big has happened to all of us. Something has disrupted our routines and changed the way we live and see the world. It's been bad, but it hasn't been all bad, so now, as some of our friends and family are receiving the vaccine and we can all start thinking about getting back to normal, I hope you'll first take some time to think about the parts of normal you hope to never get back to.

That's important to think about because experience tells me that unless I make a point of changing, I'll just go back to being the same person I was, living my life the same way I did before. Unless I try, I'll fall into the routines of traffic and rushing. I'll just go back to being overcommitted even though being less committed has been so good for me. I'll forget because that's what people do, and so, I ask you: How has this strange time changed you for the better? What will you do to keep yourself from reverting back to the way you were before?

While I don't imagine that any of us will ever look back on this year nostalgically, what's true is that some events call us, not to the same road we're used to, but to journey by a different road. That's the route the Magi took.

Our second Scripture lesson ended with the verse, "And having been warned in a dream not to return to Herod, they left for their own country by another road." Considering everything we've been through and are still going through, what new road might we be called to? That's my question for you today, on this Sunday we call Epiphany. Today, we remember when these wise visitors gave gifts to the Christ Child. I'm deliberately not saying there were three of them because we know not their number, just the number of their gifts. I'm also not saying that they were all wise men because there must have been some wise women among them, considering how they stopped in Jerusalem to ask for directions.

Our Gospel lesson begins: "In the time of King Herod, after Jesus was born in Bethlehem of Judea, they came to Jerusalem, asking, "Where is the child who has been born king of the Jews? For we observed his star at its rising, and have come to pay him homage."

We know that part.

Listen closely to this too: "When King Herod heard this, he was frightened."

We know about what happened next.

We know what he did.

It's hard to even say out loud.

He said he also wanted to pay the child homage, though really, he wanted Him destroyed. I ask you to consider both reactions, the reaction of the wise and the reaction of the King because while some encounter the miraculous and allow it to change them forever, we can all be too stubborn to change, fighting to keep things the way that they are or once were. While some manage to open themselves up to change, others fight to put life's genies back into their bottles. While some see something that makes them stop, take stock of their lives, and adapt, others live unexamined lives that lead to death and destruction. While the wise offered Him gifts of gold, frankincense, and myrrh, then left for their own country by another road, Herod would sooner kill every male child in the region than lose a grip on his power. These are two options, and as things open back up over the next few months, we'll also have to choose whose example we'll follow.

Our world has forever been changed by, not just COVID-19, but especially, the birth of the Messiah, only how will we allow these changes to change us? The wise found Him, gave Him precious gifts, and then went home by another road. On the other hand, King Herod sought Him out, and coming to terms with the truth of the Messiah's birth, was renewed in his determination not to change anything. It's the same, common event, but their reactions were so different.

It reminds me of two men, both who suffer a heart attack, but one gives thanks to God and changes his diet, the other stops for a Big Mac on the way home from the hospital. The Messiah was born, and they all knew it as we do, but the reality of His birth brought the wise men joy and made Herod afraid. Having seen Him, they left for their own country by another road, but Herod doubled down on the road he was on.

If you are listening to me this morning, then I bet that you've seen Him just as they had. This Christmas, maybe you saw Him in an act of kindness. Maybe you saw Him in the embodiment of joy, or maybe you saw Him in some experience of the holy: a healing, a miracle, a change of heart. Regardless, I'm sure that you've seen the Messiah somewhere. Now what?

Our Gospel lesson offers us two choices.

Which will it be for you?

In the last year, we've all suffered under the same fear, and we've all been frustrated by the same virus. Will this common virus enable you to see our common humanity? Will you acknowledge that just as this virus affects us all, it proves that we're not nearly so different or as divided as we've been told?

Right now, our eyes are open to the same hardships, and we've all seen such tremendous acts of kindness and sympathy that have the potential to bridge all our division. However, watch, for some will try to push us back into the same kind of partisanship we're not yet rid of, denying the reality that we truly all care about the same things. What's true is that this virus and this season has the potential to call all of us to greater unity, and the vaccine, developed in record time, reveals just what we can really do, but that well-worn road of division and indifference feels to some as comfortable as going home.

My friends, is where we were really our home?

Is a new earth not calling us?

A new realization?

A new way of being?

A new kingdom, without borders?

A new life, without old hatred?

A new realization that we are, all of us, brothers and sisters?

The world has changed over the past nine months, yet we don't have to change with it. We must choose to change. Now, in this season of New Year's Resolutions, will you, after giving the Christ Child gifts, be like those wise who "left for their own county by another road?"

Will you take some time now to think about what your Saturdays have been like, and will you fight to keep some time set aside for Sabbath rest?

Will you consider how good it has been to talk more with your brother or your sister or your mom, and will you make it a priority to keep calling them every week?

Will you remember how nice it was to have groceries delivered?

Will you rejoice in how nice life is without an hour of traffic every morning, and will you fight to keep it that way?

Will you hold close the image of a line of cars in our church parking lot, waiting to receive meals, and will you remember that our church can always make a difference to those who are in need so long as we work together?

Will you be changed, though being changed means leaving an old life behind?

Let us never go back to what was normal. Instead, let us journey with the wise by another road. Amen.

Here I Am, But Who Called Me?
1 Samuel 3: 1-10 and John 1: 43-51
Preached on January 17, 2021

Getting to know people for the first time can be a tricky business for us. On the other hand, Jesus meets Nathanael for the first time and gets him right. We meet people for the first time and think we know them, not because we're divine but because we're judgmental.

For me, it's French fries.

When I eat French fries, I eat them the right way. I make a little well of ketchup and I dip my French fries into the ketchup, which is the right way to do it. I just don't know about people who just squirt ketchup all over their fries. Likewise, my grandmother didn't think much of people who bought anything other than Duke's mayonnaise. She couldn't even understand why anyone would want to use anything else.

But there's more.

Dental hygiene, hair style, names that are hard to say or spell. We notice things and make judgments about people based on them. Additionally, we look ourselves in the mirror and make disqualifying judgements about ourselves. One thing that our two Scripture lessons for this morning have in common is that they both point out how our assumptions can lead us to miss God's invitation to new life.

Let me tell you what I mean.

A friend of mine went to school in New York State. His roommate asked him where he was from, and after Will said "Tennessee," the new roommate asked him if he owned a pair of shoes. Now that's a small thing, though being judged like that can have a big impact on a person. Interestingly, these two became friends, but they almost didn't because we think we know too much about people based on where they come from. The North looks down its nose at the South a little bit, which hurts. The South's not innocent, however. I've been making jokes about people from Alabama my entire life, and as long as "Snuffy Smith" runs in the local paper, we know that there are some people it's still socially acceptable to make fun of, only what can you really tell about a person based on where he comes from?

We can get stuck in these assumptions and start thinking that nothing good can come out of certain places or from certain people, and so we say things like, "Nazareth? Can anything good come out of Nazareth?"

Is that not the most incredible question you've ever heard?

It sums up all these assumptions and proves them wrong in one fell swoop: "Yes, in fact, the most good the world has ever seen comes out of Nazareth," so there. Still, what do we do with that? Well, I've heard some people call the desecration of our nation's capital the Duck Dynasty Revolution. However, putting down a group of people because of how they look or feel is not going to help put this nation back together.

What's become clear to me amidst all that broken glass is that we've now seen a very tangible sign that our nation is bitterly divided, and, regardless of which side you are standing on, do not forget to love the person on the other side. Why? Because Jesus always shows up where we least expect Him to, and if we're not ready to be surprised, we are likely to miss out altogether. What's true about humankind is that when we are sure we're right, we're usually wrong.

When we think we know, we're announcing our ignorance.

When we are completely certain, we leave no room for faith.

Therefore, the posture of Christians must be one of persistent humility. Why? Because we must be prepared for God to defy our expectations.

What did Nathanael expect? "Can anything good come out of Nazareth?" is what Nathanael asked. Well, Nathanael, with that attitude, can anything good come out of you?

That was Samuel's struggle.

He didn't think anything good could come out of him. Samuel didn't expect to be called by God. He just assumed it was old Eli calling. Why would he think that? Well, do you think he saw himself as someone whom God might need to do the next big thing? Had he not taken in all the messages from the judgmental world?

So often, those who sleep on the ground, as Samuel did on the floor of the Temple, never expect to rise above it. Having been left there by his mother, he may have come to think of himself like so much else that we leave behind and don't ever think about again. You surely know his story well enough. It's a story like so many others. It's like Harry Potter, who can't believe that he's a wizard. It's like James, who climbs into a Giant Peach. There are so many adventures that must begin with a child of God first believing that something wonderful could ever happen to the likes of him. We all must be ready for this kind of surprise, or we might miss it, and Samuel nearly did. "Samuel, Samuel," the Lord called. The irony here is that no one important ever called this boy by name.

No one called him, not even for dinner, but only to clean up after dinner.

No one called him because they wanted to see him, but because they wanted something done. Hardly anyone even took the time to know his name.

Do you know what that's like?

I don't know my garbage man's name, but God does. Who is calling this boy? He can't imagine because it's just too much, and that's the point. How will those who have been pushed around by society ever believe that God would call them by name? Should the garbage man start to think that he's garbage because the world treats him that way, God will break into his life to show him the truth, only he must have enough hope to imagine he's worthy.

"Samuel, Samuel," the Lord called. He almost missed it for doubting, certain that nothing like this could happen to someone like him. Don't be so certain.

Like Nathanael, we ask, "Can anything good come out of Nazareth?" Will we be so defined by the events of this week and the one before that we giveup on ourselves? Will we stop holding close the virtues that our nation was founded on? Will we be so shaken by this nightmare that we give up on the dream? Will we be convinced by the evidence around us that we are broken, divided, out of luck, and up a creek, or will we listen now to this call from God, "You're looking in all the wrong places, and you're listening to all the wrong voices. Listen to me as I call you to be fully who you were created to be!"?

Let us not be so narrow-minded as to judge ourselves based on what's broken.

Let us never be so foolish as to think that the only power at work in our world is humanity's vast capacity for evil.

Our eyes have been open to a level of fragility and depravity.

We're pushing closer to the edge of incivility, and to make matters worse, this week I've had homework to keep up with, too.

That's a small thing to mention, but I mention it for this reason. As I work on my doctorate, my professor has had me reading about the lives of black women like Ella Baker and Fanny Lou Hamer, who called this nation to her higher ideals, having never experienced much other than oppression, discrimination, and hunger. Fanny Lou Hamer was a sharecropper in

Mississippi. She worked for most of her life in fields, then went home to rest in shacks without enough coal for the fire, clothes for the children, or food for the table, yet she preached and preached about a freedom that she'd never had herself but somehow knew was within reach.

The Lord called out to Samuel, and do you know what the Lord did for him? He made him the great prophet who would bring order to a kingdom in chaos. I can imagine the boy hearing all this on that cold temple floor and wanting to say, "That sounds fine, but I'd really just like a blanket and a warm meal. What about a new tunic?" The Lord provided him more than he ever could have dreamed of, and this is the requirement: he never would have done it had he been sure that he was unworthy.

No one ever gets anywhere if they give up on themselves.

We will never get beyond this point we find ourselves in now if we stop fighting for a more perfect union, a city on a hill, the land of the free and the home of the brave, one nation, under God, indivisible with liberty and justice for all.

Can anything good come out of Nazareth?

More good than this world has ever seen before.

Can anything good come out of Washington?

Can anything good come out of me?

We cannot allow one of the worst days in our nation's history to determine our nation's future, any more than we can allow one of our worst mistakes to determine our salvation.

Only by the grace of God go I.

Only by the power of God did I walk into today with confidence.

Only because of His magnificence can this ordinary me stand in this pulpit.

It's only because of forgiveness, grace, love, hope, and faith that we are here today, so listen to the call of God my friends, and together, let us find out what will happen next. I'm ready to follow this Jesus Who has called me by name. He saw me under the fig tree and invited me to follow. I believe He loves me, and I believe He loves you, and I am absolutely convinced that He has not had it with this world that we are living in. In fact, I believe He holds this whole world in His hands.

Amen.

Dropping the Nets
Jonah 3: 1-5, 10 and Mark 1: 14-20
Preached on January 24, 2021

There are two aspects of this Scripture lesson from the Gospel of Mark that have become clearer to me in the last week: the first is that these disciples aren't completely unique in their willingness to drop everything. People we know are doing some version of that often enough that we ought to recognize it. All of us have likely at times done some version of the same thing, for letting go is a requirement of every disciple of Jesus Christ, not just the disciples of 2,000 years ago.

The second realization I've had in the last week thinking about this Gospel lesson is that this account is just the beginning of their letting go. In fact, following Jesus towards the Kingdom of God requires that all disciples keep on dropping important things. It may be that we have to keep on dropping nets the whole way there. Let me try to tell you what I'm really getting at.

Back in Columbia, Tennessee where we lived before moving back here to Marietta, I heard stories about young men who would hear the call of God as they worked in the tobacco fields. They'd drop what they were doing to become ministers of the Gospel; however, the county historian there once told me, "If you find that story awe inspiring, then you don't know what working in a tobacco field is like. Anyone would answer a call from God out there. A young man would say just about anything to get himself out from those endless rows of tobacco on a hot summer day. Don't be so impressed."

Of course, I am impressed. I'm impressed every time I see people doing this kind of thing, even if maybe they're not doing it for purely spiritual reasons. Still, consider: sometimes letting go of the first thing is easy, and then you keep having to do it, which makes me think of this first-hand account of a young white woman right here in Cobb County, who said that when her brother heard that Lincoln had been elected president, he rushed off to South Carolina to enlist. She was caught up in how he nearly dropped his hoe in the field to rush off to the fight; however, how was it once the war began? How was it once winter came? How was it for him coming home, questioning the cause or refusing to let it go? Sometimes, adventure calls us to let go of our nets, and we'd be fools not to listen, although we're also fools to think that's where letting go ends.

Every soldier knows that letting go of the comforts of home is just the first step in a long journey. On that journey, some let go of their very humanity. The path of discipleship is the same in the sense that we have to keep letting go, day after day, again and again, but the path of discipleship is one of stepping closer to the Kingdom: dying to self, dying to ego, dying to comfort, to take up a cross. For disciples who are letting go to follow Christ, it's worth it because every time we let go of something like our nets, every time we suffer for the sake of Him, we're stepping out of darkness and towards the light.

I heard about it in an audio book I was listening to with the woman who runs First Presbyterian Church, Melissa Ricketts. Her official title here is Director of Administration, and you may know that Melissa Ricketts and I rode down to South Georgia last Saturday. Representing all of you, representing this church, we were there at the graveside with Rev. Joe Brice and his wife, Sandra, as they buried their son. It was hard to be there; however, we wouldn't have been anywhere else, only we had to get there first, and the getting there took a long time. It was about five hours down and five hours back. It was one of those drives where you come off the interstate and think you're getting close, but you're not.

The day before, when I was just getting ready to go, our daughters were worried about me being a passenger in Melissa's car. They were very concerned that I might not be an engaging enough passenger in the car of one of their favorite people. They feel as though I can be a boring person to ride in the car with, so they suggested I bring a book to listen to on the way, and I did. My wife, Sara, made the recommendation having read it already. This book, it's called *The Love Story of Missy Carmichael*, is the story of a woman who lost her husband and never changed a thing in their house.

You can imagine.

The story starts moving when she meets a friend who comes over and, describing the place as a mausoleum, offers to help her sort through it all. Sorting through the stuff was an emotional experience for Missy Carmichael because letting go of all that stuff was like letting go of her husband all over again. It was hard for her to do, yet once she started letting go of what was there, she noticed the light coming through the windows.

I tell you about this book because it makes this clear.

It makes it clear how hard it is to let go, but also how pure the light is.

That's what discipleship is like.

We let go of our nets, but from letting go, something happens.

Real life starts again.

Joy comes.

We're not trapped in a perpetual cycle of the way things are.

It's the opposite of the TV show *Hoarders*. Do you know that show? Sometimes that show can hit a little too close to home. I haven't watched the show in a while; I don't know if it's still even on, but what I remember is how often, for the people on that show, the physical stuff wasn't just stuff, and letting it go was so painful they almost couldn't do it. It's like Mrs. Havisham in the book *Great Expectations*. We who watch want to say, "Get out of that old wedding dress," only she can't take it off, and neither can she get on with living.

Likewise, down in our basement are my old baseball cards.

Up in the attic are yearbooks from high school.

Our girls were rummaging around in my sock drawer, and they wanted to know why I had a Ziploc bag filled with little teeth.

I'll tell you why.

It's because it's hard to let go.

It's hard to let kids grow up.

It's hard to say goodbye to who they were and what we had.

It's hard to move on.

Sometimes, it's hard to get on with living because living requires letting go.

Letting go, over and over.

Letting something go.

At the beginning of this sermon, I said that people like us do it all the time, and they do, and so often it's worth it. Have you ever seen a woman who let go of everything to become a mother? The disciples letting go of their nets must have been something like that. Some of you have been that woman who let go of everything to pick up a tiny bundle of life and made that bundle the center of everything. You let go to let the light in. You can't imagine doing anything else, but did you know that you were going to have to keep letting go? Did you know that you were going to have to let go of her hands so she could walk? Did you know that you were going to have to let go of her so she could go off to college?

Fathers are bad at all of this. It takes us too long to let go of ourselves at the beginning, and then we almost can't bear to do let go of our children in the end. I remember how Sara became a mother the first second she held Lily in her arms. It happened right before my eyes. She just let go of self-centeredness and made her daughter the center of her whole world, while I was still the same self-centered guy that I was the day before. I was ready to leave the hospital because I was kind of ready to get back home so I could watch TV and take a nap as though my whole life hadn't been transformed. Now I watch as fathers walk their daughters down the aisle to let them go, and I have an idea of how long it will take me to recover from doing that, only I also know that this is what I signed up for. This is what life requires, and discipleship isn't any different.

We have to keep letting go so that more light can come in.

You know what happens to people from the TV show *Hoarders* who can't let go, but there's an even worse warning for those who hold on and don't let the light in. It's there in the book of Jonah. We don't always get really deep into the full story of Jonah and the whale. We simplify it because this is a story we tell children, so kids grow up thinking that the hard to believe part of the story is that a man could get swallowed by a whale then spit up on a beach three days later. That's not the hardest part to believe. The hardest part for Jonah to believe is that God would want to save the Assyrians.

That sounds silly if you don't know how awful the Assyrians were.

They were demonic.

Had they been the ones to march on Capitol Hill, they'd make what we saw two weeks ago look like a yard sale or a lemonade stand. When they invaded a nation, they would skin their enemies alive. They'd burn children, destroy cities, enslave survivors, and God wanted Jonah to go preach to them. That's a terrifying proposition, but it got worse. When Jonah finally did, they listened.

Those Assyrians were like so many disciples.

They let go of who they were and became someone new, which surely brought an awful lot of light into their lives. However, Jonah wasn't ready for it to happen because he couldn't let go of the hatred he was holding onto. You know how disappointed Jonah was. He pouted under that broom tree. Then God sent a worm and killed the tree. In our first Scripture lesson, it sounds like he just being a big baby, only we can't simplify his disappointment, or we'll miss the point. He was disappointed because his whole life he'd been dreaming of the moment God would wipe these enemies of his from the face of the earth, then God wants him to let go of that dream to face a new reality.

Do you know how hard that is?

This is something that some people are never able to do.

They can't see what's right in front of them as good because it's not the good that they wanted to see. They can't tell that it's a blessing because it's not the blessing that they had asked for. Disappointment breaks their hearts. It happens all the time. Again and again, we must let go of what we wanted to happen, what we thought would bring the light in, to trust that God might know better than we do.

The persistent call of Christ is, "drop what you're holding onto," and follow Me. Don't let that call sound too easy, or you're fooling yourself. It's not easy, but don't let that call sound impossible either. People do it all the time, and they can tell you that doing so lets more light in. C.S. Lewis said it was something like a child, happily making mud pies in an alleyway, receiving an invitation to the beach. She's never been to the beach. She can't imagine the beach, but when we let go of what we know, we stand to gain what might be.

When we let go of bitterness, we stand to gain joy.

When we let go of hatred, we stand to gain love.

When we let go of our nets, we stand to be a part of the transformation of this whole planet.

Let go of your nets.

Let go of what was.

Follow Christ towards the light.

Amen.

As One Having Authority
Deuteronomy 18: 15-20 and Mark 1: 21-28
Preached on January 31, 2021

In this second Scripture lesson from the Gospel of Mark, Jesus is described twice "as one having authority." Wouldn't you like for people to describe you that way? How could I get our children to describe me that way? At our house, it's like I'm Rodney Dangerfield: "I don't get no respect!" so how do we get it? The answer is there in the passage.

When a man with an unclean spirit cried out to Him, "What have you to do with us, Jesus of Nazareth? Have you come to destroy us?" Jesus rebuked the spirit saying, "Be silent," and then commanded the spirit to "come out," and it did. His words had power because they weren't empty. He said, "come out" to the unclean spirit, and it did, so if he told you, "Take out the garbage or you're grounded," you knew He was serious, and if He said He loved you, it was clear He meant it.

What, then, is the difference between Him and the rest?

Why is it worth mentioning that He spoke as one having authority?

What's the difference between Jesus and all the empty suits and windbags, whose words we hear but know we can't take to the bank?

Here's the difference: He actually does what everyone else just talked about doing.

To Him, it's not just words.

It was never just speech.

If Jesus were to run for president, you could take all His campaign promises, not with a grain of salt but knowing that He was as good as His word. There haven't been many presidents like that. In fact, some historians say that there was only one. People in Columbia, Tennessee are glad to tell you who it was. Every citizen of Columbia is happy to tell you all about it because this great town south of Nashville where we lived before moving back here to Marietta is especially proud of James K. Polk, the 11th President of the United States, who lived there.

President Polk was actually born in North Carolina, but don't try to tell anyone in Columbia, Tennessee that. They're not interested in where the man was born. He was from Columbia, and while he was running for president, he lived in a house that's now right across the street from the Presbyterian Church. Folks are proud of that, so the Presbyterians in Columbia are quick to tell you that the *K* in James K. Polk stands for Knox, for he was a direct descendant of that great Scottish leader of the Presbyterian Church, John Knox, but the Methodists will be quick to tell you that he had a deathbed conversion and became a Methodist.

Now, this is true, even though it sounds like it couldn't be.

The first time I was in the First United Methodist Church in Columbia, I looked closely at the great rose window in their sanctuary. It's a beautiful stained-glass window, but I did a double take the first time I saw it because I expected it to be Jesus in the center. He's not; it's the 11th President, James K. Polk, whom the Methodists claim as one of their own. Now, what's the point of me telling you all this? I'll tell you. A close friend of mine, Tom Price, was one of the historians on staff at the Polk Home, and when Tom was giving his standard speech on President Polk, as he was often called on to do, he would always say that Polk only made four campaign promises:

1. To expand the borders of our country, which he did through the acquisition of the Oregon Territory, California, New Mexico, and settling the Texas border dispute.

2. To lower tariffs, which he did.

3. The establishment of a new federal depository system, done in four years.

4. And the strengthening of the executive office, mission accomplished.

Many historians will say that he left office at the end of this first term not seeking reelection, and as the most successful president since George Washington. Anyone is Columbia, Tennessee will tell you that he left office as the most successful president of all time, and I'll agree with them because he did what he said he would do.

It's amazing.

Is that not amazing?

Is it not also amazing that we think living up to campaign promises is amazing?

Why have we grown used to accepting false hope, half-truths, and good tries? I don't know, but when people heard Jesus, they were impressed, and when they saw how He lived, they knew that He teaches as "one having authority." He's not like the scribes who just talk about the Scriptures; He's actually living them. He's not going for personal glory; He wants to glorify His Father in Heaven. He wasn't all talk and no action. His words had authority because of His actions. It's a rare thing to find a president like that; it's a gift to find a person like that, and unfortunately, the world has seen far too many churches who were just too good at saying one thing while doing another.

I've been talking about presidents, but this event in the life of Jesus described in our second Scripture lesson doesn't take place in town hall or Congress. It's an exorcism that takes place, not in a place where people do political things, but in one of those places where people worship: a synagogue. The place where all people are supposed to be welcome; however, let's be honest, not everyone always is. Verse 23 makes it plain who belonged there and who didn't: "Just then there was in their synagogue a man with an unclean spirit," as though the synagogue belonged to those who had it all together and not those who needed a little help.

"Their" synagogue?

Whose synagogue?

Is it not always God's synagogue, where sinners like us are always welcome?

Was this place and so many others like it not created to be a place of prayer for all people?

The Pope was clear a few years ago: "The church is a field hospital for the sick," but how often is it more like a place for the upright to gather together away from the rest of the world? How often have you invited someone to church to hear them say, "I'm not sure I belong there?" Who does belong here, and who doesn't? I don't know, so something we try to make clear Sunday after Sunday is that sinners are welcome. The broken are embraced. Those who hold their heads too high or think they have it all together really have no need for what we have to offer, for what good is grace to the perfect, and who needs forgiveness but those who have made a mistake?

Every Sunday, we pray a prayer of confession.

That's a countercultural thing to do.

Sometimes, I can't believe that we do it, but we do. Sunday after Sunday, we pray it all together. Today, it went like this:

Most merciful God, I sing, "May Jesus Christ be praised!"

But I confess that through my words and actions, Jesus Christ is not always praised.

Forgive me, Lord, for while I worship you in the company of the upright, too often I stoop down to the level of the self-centered and self-righteous.

We say words like that in here, and we know they're true, yet we also have to live them.

What good does it do us or anyone else if we come to worship God and confess our imperfection, then live our whole week according to a standard of perfection rather than a standard of grace?

What good does it do us or anyone else if we make plain our faults before God then hide our faults away as soon as we get back to living?

What good does it do the world if we aren't constantly proclaiming a gospel of forgiveness in a culture of "three strikes and you're out?"

What good is this faith of ours if it doesn't change the way we live, if it doesn't change the way we see ourselves, if it doesn't change the way we treat each other?

There was a man in the synagogue with an unclean spirit, and he cried out, "What have you to do with us, Jesus of Nazareth? Have you come to destroy us?" That's how it feels to a whole lot of people. What have you to do with me, church lady; have you come to judge me? What are you doing here, preacher? Have you come to make me feel guilty? What are you doing here, Jesus? Have you come to destroy us? You know the answer.

For God so loved the world that he gave his only Son, so that everyone who believes in him may not perish but may have eternal life. Indeed, God did not send the Son into the world to condemn the world, but in order that the world might be saved through him.

Those are good words.

A lot of people have them memorized, only they don't matter unless we live them.

We are too often those without any authority because too often we don't live the faith that we profess. We fight over who gets to put the President's name on their church's membership roll, and we don't know what to do when less-prestigious members of society walk through our doors. I've seen it. I've been a part of it, and often, it's the least of these who reveal who we truly are. Do you remember the last time it happened here?

Rev. Cassie Waits was giving the benediction.

This was a long time ago when a whole bunch of people were able to come and sit in this room. Along with everyone else was a man who was about to be evicted. He interrupted Cassie while she was giving the benediction and announced to this whole church, "I need some help," in a loud voice. For a few, long seconds, no one knew what to do. Presbyterians don't even clap, much less shout in the middle of a worship service, so I walked up to him and was walking him out of our church. As I walked up that aisle, you started slipping money into my hands. By the time we were out the door, there was enough to pay three months' rent, which was nothing short of a miracle, but I'm telling you this story today because it was in that moment that I knew fully who we are. It was the man with an unclean spirit who saw Jesus for Who He was, and it was the man who shouted out his need in the middle of aworship service who revealed the heart of this congregation.

He knew us.

He revealed our identity.

He reminded us of who we are and what we were created to be.

For that reason and many others, I am daily so proud to serve this church. It is a constant gift to walk through these doors, and when people ask me who I am and what I do, I tell them, "My name is Joe Evans, and I am proud to serve First Presbyterian Church as one of her pastors." Then they'll say, as they did at the school board about a year ago, "Yours is the church who has made a difference to so many children through Club 3:30," or "I've seen the wall of pictures of all the Habitat Houses y'all built," or more recently, "Thank you for feeding so many families by giving them food in your parking lot." You see, the world around us knows us not by what we say. We only have authority when our words and our actions match up.

May it always be so.

Amen.

From Transfiguration to Easter

This next sermon begins Jesus' long journey to the Cross. From the Mount of Transfiguration, He goes step-by-step towards His death and then beyond it. It is truly a comfort to know that He has already been all the places we must go. During the season of Lent, as we take up that annual discipline of fasting and going without, we remember how He journeys beside us, leading us through our lives and beyond.

One Foot in Front of the Other
2nd Kings 2: 1-12 and Mark 9: 2-9
Preached on February 14, 2021

Both our first and second Scripture lessons take place on top of a mountain. Both are momentous occasions, which makes sense to me because some of the momentous occasions of my life have also taken place on mountaintops. The first time Sara kissed me, we were up on top of a mountain. I proposed to her a couple years later on that same mountain peak, and because she said yes, even more so, I think of mountaintops as meaningful places. As you can imagine, that day I was nervous on our way up, working up the courage to ask. At the top, I felt relief and joy when she said, "yes," but then, as we went back down it was clear that I suddenly had a whole new set of things to be nervous about that I hadn't even really considered on the way up. I hadn't really thought about how much growing up is required of making that step from being someone's boyfriend to being her husband.

Maybe this is true of mountains: we're expecting the challenge of gettingto the top of them, only what about the coming down? Sometimes mountaintops change us, so going down the mountain, I remember how she was talking about telling our friends and her family: dates and location of the ceremony. Where would we live? What would happen next? Nervous the whole way up that mountain, I expected to be more relaxed coming back down, but I wasn't because on top of that mountain everything had changed, and now, we were on our way to some place new that I'd never been to before.

Do you know what that's like, finding yourself on the way to some place new because you are someone new?

You have to rethink whom you are closest to and which relationship are the most important? Thinking about mountaintops, how do you come back down? How do you re-integrate yourself into the world as a changed person? I suppose one way to do it is to learn from people who have done it before. You noticed that Jesus isn't alone in our second Scripture lesson; Moses makes his way into this event that we call the Transfiguration from the Gospel of Mark. You know all about Moses, and this is what occurs to me about Moses today, as he appears, dazzling white, beside Jesus up on top of that mountain: he'd already led the people out of Egypt and across the sea, but it's only when coming down from a mountaintop having received the Ten Commandments from Almighty God that we see how he's changed, while the Hebrew people are busy building an idol out of gold, as though they'd never really left Egypt.

Has it ever been this way with you?

Have you ever noticed that something was different inside of you, something had changed?

That you were not the same, and you no longer fit in with those you used to fit in with because suddenly you'd been transformed?

In this season of mask-wearing and physical distancing, surely we're all feeling a little of that still. I preached a funeral for a long-time church member, Joan Young, last Saturday, and the funeral home staff member said that they've had four times as many funerals last month than they did January of last year. For some of us, everything has changed because of this virus, but then you get around certain people who act as though nothing's changed.

How do you handle that?

How do we handle the change that takes place within us, even as the rest of the world is slow to change?

Moses knew what it was like and so did Elisha.

There are two prophets in our first Scripture lesson with dangerously similar sounding names: Elijah and Elisha. Elijah is there with Moses in our second Scripture lesson up on top of the mountain with Jesus, so maybe you know a lot about him already. What about Elisha? In our first Scripture lesson, Elijah and Elisha make their way up a mountain. On their way to the mountain, Elijah took his mantle, rolled it up, and struck the Jordan River so that the water was parted to the one side and to the other. Together, they walked through the water on dry land as Moses and the Hebrew people did through the sea, but then they went to the top of the mountain, and Elijah was taken up into Heaven by a whirlwind. Elisha had to go back down the mountain as a changed man, walking into an unchanged world, now without the person who'd always shown him the way.

Do you know what that's like, taking a most important step, without anyone to hold your hand?

I feel sure that you do.

Last week, we had a special church-staff lunch to celebrate Alesia Jones and her ministry among us. Her parents were there, and her father told me that he still remembered how brave she was walking across the stage at a large auditorium, nothing on the stage but his ten-year-old girl and a grand piano she intended to play in front of this huge crowd. This is how it is. To grow, we take steps into the unknown, without always having someone by our side, and sometimes it's even taking a step into the valley of the shadow of death.

Jesus led the disciples up the mountain, then started back down.

Where was he going?

You know, and so did Peter.

Peter didn't like it.

Of course, he didn't.

Something that's funny to think about is how many leaders we know of will do anything to hold onto their power and influence. Some will fight tooth and nail to be re-elected, or they keep going to the office long after they should. They can't pass leadership to anyone new, while Jesus spends this huge part of his ministry trying to get Peter to lead, and Peter won't do it. Peter doesn't want to come down from the mountain. He's not ready to take the next step. He says to Jesus, up on top of that mountain, "Rabbi, it is good for us to be here; let us make three dwellings, one for you, one for Moses, and one for Elijah." It's as though he's saying, "There's no reason for us to go back down. Let's just stay right up here. It's just us. We're fine. We'll make some dwellings, James will start a fire, and John will gather some pinecones or something for us to eat. Let's just stay right up here for a while because I'm not ready to take the next step. I'm not ready to leave this place. I'm not ready for us to go any further. I'm fine where I am."

Do you know that feeling?

Sure, you do.

Everyone does.

It's the feeling we've been having since we were babies. We took our first step, and as soon as it's done being exciting, we wanted to be back in our mother's arms. We remember how Peter wants to walk on the water, only then he looks down and starts to sink. "Help me, Jesus!" he yelled, and Jesus did, but what's going to happen when Jesus isn't there to bail him out?

For Peter, this moment up on top of the mountain brings with it this horrible realization: that all the time Jesus has been talking about being the Son of God, He was serious. That when He said He had to go on to Jerusalem to fulfill His purpose, He wasn't joking, and that when Jesus had been talking about His death, He meant it.

What that means for Peter is that his old life is over.

His true purpose is right on the horizon, and any doubts he has within himself might as well be left behind on the mountaintop.

The time for playing at being the Rock of the Church has come to an end, and the time to be the Rock of the Church is coming because Jesus is going to Jerusalem to die.

How do you cope with that?

How do you become someone new?

How do you walk into the unknown without the person who's always been there?

That's an important question for us to ask ourselves today, as Alesia Jones, who's been on that rug for our kids all through this pandemic, and for so many years before that, is moving on to make a difference in this world in new and different ways. She's made a difference to our kids, and now she's leaving. How do we cope with that?

I ask that question as a parent.

You might imagine that our daughters have received several Bibles in their lives. They have. People give Bibles to preacher's kids, but the only Bibles I've seen them read voluntarily are the Bibles Alesia Jones gave them. She's been leading all our children on their journeys of faith for 22 years now. And because she's retiring, I call your attention to this truth: that the very best leaders are those who teach us how to stand on our own.

The journey is long.

The path is rarely easy.

Yet, God gives us companions on the journey, and the best of those companions aren't always there to hold our hands. The very best are those who show us that we have the strength within us to step out on our own. Step-by-step, we walk down the mountain, not always to the sound of applause and a supportive crowd, but sometimes to shouts and jeers. When that happens, we cannot cease being transformed, though the world remains the same. We must be a part of the transformation of this entire world.

Challenge after challenge.

Change after change.

Doing, not what's easy, but what' right.

Not what's popular, but what's true.

Moving towards the Promised Land, not like sheep without a shepherd, but like disciples, who have made the faith of their mothers and fathers their own.

Thank you, Alesia Jones, for walking with my children, and for helping them along their journey. Thank you, on behalf of so many parents and so many children of this church. We are all better because of you, and we will continue on.

Amen.

A Sermon for Ash Wednesday
2nd Corinthians 5: 20b – 6:2
Preached on February 17, 2021

I'll begin this Ash Wednesday sermon with three riddles: two you probably know the answer to because you've heard them before. The third, maybe not because I just made it up:

What grows the more you take away from it?

A hole.

What hides in the light but is killed by the darkness?

A shadow.

What obstacle is insurmountable, only so long as you're unwilling to face it?

Whatever you think separates you from the love of God.

I don't know if that's a good riddle or not, but I do believe it's true.

This evening, our Scripture lesson is an invitation to reconciliation: "Be reconciled to God," Paul writes, only here's the thing: according to a New Testament scholar Paul Sampley, "This is the only place in [all of Paul's letters] where the reconciling is to be done by us."

He's right. Think about one of the greatest chapters in the entire Bible, Romans 8:

For I am convinced that neither death, nor life, nor angels, nor rulers, nor things present, nor things to come, nor powers, nor height, nor depth, nor anything else in all creation, will be able to separate us from the love of God in Christ Jesus our Lord.

Do you know that one?

I think it's the best, and it is because it's true. Still, let me ask this question: what are you convinced can separate you from the love of God?

What are you convinced makes you unlovable?

What are you sure has you on the list of those who will never make it through the gates of Heaven?

What have you done that invalidates you, condemns you, excludes you, or vilifies you?

Lurking in our subconscious is this fear that keeps us from facing the truth, so I've heard of people who have gone years without opening up their credit card bills; people who have never checked their cholesterol; and those who ignore their check engine lights.

Guess how that works out for them.

Consider people who lie and lie and lie, not just to avoid the consequences of their actions, but to fool themselves into thinking that they haven't done anything wrong. When we don't have the courage to look sin in the face, the Devil has us right where he wants us because a sin that we're afraid to face has complete power over us.

Obstacles between us and God are only obstacles when we're afraid to confess them.

We deny ourselves forgiveness, only when we can't force ourselves to confess.

Tonight, we must take sin's power over us away.

We must not hide it in the shadow where it grows.

We can't numb our pain with denial.

We have to summon the courage to look it in the eye, and as soon as we do, it shrinks down to nothing.

Let me tell you what I mean.

Today, as we all work to process what happened January 6th on Capitol Hill, the voices I'm hearing might be divided into two simple categories: those who would support the President, should he try to pardon himself, and those who would wipe his memory from the history books. At this point, I just can't stand it any longer. I can no longer tolerate the thought of raising our daughters in a world where there are only two options for an imperfect person to choose between. Today, I am reminding myself that the Church has always offered a third option, and it is offered to us each week. Sunday after Sunday, something countercultural happens at First Presbyterian Church and so many places of worship like it. Upstanding people make a public confession of sin. These days, many of us do it virtually, but it's still a crucial part of the service because we all need it. We all need the freedom to admit to ourselves and to our God that we aren't perfect.

In our daily living, we go with the crowd and get swept away.

We fail to speak, or we say the wrong thing.

We do harm to ourselves and to our brothers and sisters, both intentionally and unintentionally. Typically, it sounds like this:

Merciful God, we confess that we have sinned against you in thought, word, and deed, by what we have done, and by what we have left undone. In your mercy, forgive what we have been, help us amend what we are, and direct what we shall be.

In other words, every Sunday, I have the chance to face the facts, to accept the consequences, and to become someone better. As a pastor who now serves in the same church in which I was raised, every time I stand before the congregation, I celebrate the grace that has allowed me to step beyond my wayward teenage years and to become someone different.

I face the consequences of my actions, but I'm washed in grace.

I'm allowed to face the truth of who I am without being cast out or exiled.

I'm persistently invited to become someone different, and so I can't tolerate how our society only offers two options: pardon or expulsion.

Thanks be to God, there is a third: We can openly say we were wrong, we can face the consequences, and we can receive forgiveness.

That's really what I believe would heal our nation right now, and so I wish that the President would confess to his role in inciting the mob. That's the example I want our daughters to see. I want to shield their eyes from the cycle of denial, blame, and excuses. As they come to know themselves as those who inherit an imperfect nation, I wish that they might see President Trump admit his imperfection and pledge to do better. It's this kind of courage to confess that we, the people of the United States of America, should ask of our leaders because that's all that we can ask of ourselves.

As followers of Jesus Christ, we often worry over the absence of Biblical values in government and society. If there were just one such value for us to reclaim today, it is that which is presented by the Parable of the Prodigal Son.

Seeing how much harm he has done to himself and his community, the son humbly makes his way back home. Not expecting or deserving mercy, walking under the heavy truth of his imperfection, he is embraced by his father and surrounded by his love.

Such a gift is offered to us all.

May you never forget it because we all need it, and our God persistently offers it.

Our God does not dismiss or reject us but provides for His children a way to be made clean once more.

Our nation is not perfect, but the road to a more perfect union is not paved by rejecting those who fall *or* by hiding from the truth. When we reject those whose brokenness is obvious, we are not removing the sin from our own hearts, we are just removing another sinner from our midst. Therefore, let usall seek that more perfect union that our forefathers and foremothers dreamed of by admitting our faults and pledging to be better:

Merciful God, I confess that I have sinned against you in thought, word, and deed. My ego silenced my virtue, and I couldn't accept defeat. Rather than heal division, I aggravated it. Rather than serve the common good, I served myself. Rather than face the old national demons: lies, racism, and selfishness, they danced on the capitol because I'm still working to exercise them from my heart. In your mercy, forgive what I have been, help me amend what I am, and direct who I shall be.

Amen.

Divine Things and Human Things
Genesis 17: 1-7, 15-16 and Mark 8: 31-38
Preached on February 28, 2021

Last Thursday, the front page of the *Marietta Daily Journal* featured the headline, "Kennesaw Church Expelled." Such a headline made the front page because the Towne View Baptist Church was "kicked out of the Southern Baptist Convention."

This was a painful article to read for a number of reasons. One of those reasons was self-centered, for as a pastor, I felt sorry for the pastor of that church who said, "this is kind of like hearing from your family that you don't belong anymore." Still, I felt sorrier for the family who found themselves at the center of this controversy. They are a couple with three adopted children who just wanted a church to belong to and not a denominational schism. Then, at the same time I felt pride and admiration because this church exemplifies the Gospel call in a particular way. Maybe like you, I know that sometimes a church must make a hard decision. Whenever a church chooses to embody the love of Jesus Christ, even if it costs them the approval of a governing body, I rejoice because I believe in doing so, they make the cost of discipleship plain.

Following Jesus costs something.

Doing the right thing often costs something.

The Lord Himself makes the cost of discipleship absolutely plain in this second Scripture lesson from the Gospel of Mark.

For any who struggle to see that the Christian faith promises a cross and not a Cadillac, listen to this:

Then he began to teach them that the Son of Man must undergo great suffering, and be rejected by the elders, the chief priests, and the scribes, and be killed, and after three days rise again. He said all this quite openly. And Peter took him aside and began to rebuke him.

Why did Peter rebuke him?

Why did Peter take Jesus aside?

It's because Peter didn't want Jesus to be that kind of Messiah.

Peter didn't think that suffering and rejection had anything to do with being the Messiah.

In a world of comfort, quick fixes, and simplified solutions, who would follow a Messiah Who suffers? Peter wanted a nice, quiet Messiah Who would be everyone's hero. He wanted Jesus to be that someone everyone could cheer on in a great parade. A Savior and Friend Who would one day retire with him to the beach, and together Peter and Jesus could look back on all their years of ministry and Peter would say to his Friend in the beach chair next to him, "Jesus, it's been a wonderful life, hasn't it?"

Maybe there was a part of Jesus that wanted this kind of life, too, so He must rebuke Peter just as He rebuked the Devil back in the wilderness: "Get behind me, Satan!" he said to his friend, "for you are setting your mind not on divine things but on human things."

Isn't it easy to set your mind on human things?

Isn't it easy to get all caught up in what everyone thinks?

Not everyone does, though, or not everyone does all the time.

When the great evangelist Rev. Billy Graham died, I remembered one of his most famous quotes: "My home is in Heaven. I'm just passing through this world." That was him, maybe on a good day. For the rest of us, it's easy to get stuck in this world.

Isn't it easy to set your mind on human things?

A Puritan prayer book that I love says it this way: "O Savior of Sinners, raise me above the smiles and frowns of the world, regarding it as a light thing to be judged by humans."

Do you know anyone who needs to pray that prayer?

I know I need it.

Maybe you do, too.

In this strange time of COVID-19, isn't a prayer like that one what we all need?

Parents have to help their children make even more difficult decisions than ever because now, when your son finally makes the basketball team, you have to decide whether or not to even let him play. Is loving our kids letting them do something that makes them feel normal or is loving them better embodied in going lengths to keep them safe and behind masks? In every single decision, we must weigh options like these. We must constantly ask ourselves: "How do I protect myself; how do I protect my children; how can I keep them from being social outcasts when I'm constantly faced with mollifying one group of people but disappointing another?"

How can we even speak anymore?

These days, obvious statements, like "Black lives matter," carry with them not just the undeniable value of human life, but allegiance to a particular group and a particular way of seeing the world.

You know this struggle.

It's a fool's errand to try and walk the middle path, agonizing over appearances, working to appease everyone, though I've been that fool again and again and again, and I bet you have, too. You lean one way, and you're someone's hero but someone else's enemy, and it sure does feel like you're dying a slow death if you are unable to rise above the smiles and frowns of the world. It's impossible for you to regard it as a light thing to be judged by humans if your mind is set on human things.

Jesus said to Peter, "You are setting your mind not on divine things but on human things," and if that's the way we choose to live, persistently attempting to gain the approval of the crowd, the denomination, or the neighborhood, then it's going to be nothing but torture from here on out.

It was that way for me in my first year of ministry.

I began my ministry at Good Shepherd Presbyterian Church out in Lilburn, GA, and I was going to be everything to everybody even if it killed me. Someone asked me if I liked to listen to *The Fish* – that Christian radio station, and so I started to listen to it, even though I hated it. A group wanted to start a Bible study, and so I helped them get it going; then another group wanted one, then another, and before long I was leading a Bible study every day of the week, listening to *The Fish* in the car. There was no place of solace because I was trying to please someone everywhere I went. Basically, the hardest thing about my first year of ministry was that I was trying to be, not the pastor who I was, not the pastor God created me to be, but the pastor who I thought they wanted me to be.

Then one morning, I woke up with a rash on my stomach. It started out red and itchy, and it wouldn't go away. Sara finally sent me to the doctor. He told me that it was hives, and that he could give me some medicine for it, but really it was just from stress, and what I needed to do was find a way to relax.

"You're a preacher, right?" my doctor asked.

I told him that I was, and so he said again, "What you need to do is find a way to relax. Have you ever heard of prayer?"

What is prayer, but the opportunity to remember again that our identity and our value comes not from humans but from God; that our primary relationship must be between our Creator and us.

To quote that great prayer for illumination: "Lord, among all the changing words of this generation, speak to us your eternal Word, which does not change." We pray this prayer because it is God's voice that defines us, not the whispers of the gossips or the pressure to conform.

Jesus did ask his disciples, "Who do they say that I am?" though the difference between Him asking this question and us asking the same is that He didn't really care who anybody said He was. He already knew.

For us, it takes a little more work and a constant willingness to try and remember.

We all have to slow down and accept it.

We all have to listen for it because it's right there for us.

Rather than speed up to try and earn it or buckle down to feel like we've gotten there, we have to silence the crowd whispering in our ears that we might listen to His voice because we'll never get there, and we won't find rest until we rest in God and who God says we are.

In our baptism, the Lord told us all about who we are: "You are mine, my beloved, and with you I am well pleased." The difference between all of us and Jesus is that He never forgot it. He was always bold to believe it, and He never depended on humans to tell Him Who He was or how He should live.

Let our prayer be: "O Savior of Sinners, raise me above the smiles and frowns of the world, regarding it as a light thing to be judged by humans," and may our song be like that great but lesser-known hymn, "How Clear Is Our Vocation, Lord:"

If worldly pressures fray the mind,

And love itself cannot unwind

Its tangled skein of care;

Our inward life repair.

For how will we make it to the Kingdom of Heaven, if deep in our hearts, we long for the approval of this broken world? We must set our minds, not on human things, but on divine things. Therefore, as you wrestle with the great balancing act of life in the 21st Century, know that those who choose love, no matter what it costs, live with far more joy in their lives than those who have gained the approval of this world.

That preacher who is no longer a Southern Baptist, said it like this, "This little church in Kennesaw, we paid a price to do it, [but I'm not willing to tell people], 'God made you, but God hates you because of how you are,' so I'm not going to do it anymore." I wish we all could be so brave because with such willingness to face rejection in the name of love, we choose the path that Christ chose for Himself.

In order to really live, we all must rise above the smiles and frowns of the world to follow Him. To truly follow, we must leave the approval of this broken world behind. We must live so that, in us, they catch a glimpse of the reign of love and mercy that is to come.

Doing so has never been easy.

It won't ever be easy.

Listen to this, though: while most preachers settled into a society of segregation, there was one who gave his life for the cause, and this is what he had to say:

For years now I have heard the word "Wait!"...This "Wait" has almost always meant "Never." [So] We must come to see...that "justice too long delayed is justice denied."

Likewise, love too long delayed is love denied.

We all must be so bold as to risk what we have to love people better.

For who was Abraham but one who gave up his present circumstance to be a part of God's great plan?

Who was Dr. King but one who gave his life for the sake of a dream?

Who was Christ but one Who chose to be rejected by the powers and principalities of Rome that He might open His arms wide, showing all generations that there is a power stronger than fear or death?

Let us follow Him, risking something, but gaining everything.

Amen.

Braid the Whip
Malachi 3: 1-7 and John 2: 13-22
Preached on March 7, 2021

One of the shortest verses in the Bible, "Jesus wept," and another like it, "Jesus laughed," despite brevity, tell us so much about this Savior of ours, whose emotional life we are prone to reduce down to some kind of warm, solemn piety.

You can see what I'm talking about in art.

Some of us grew up in Sunday school rooms with paintings of Jesus on the wall that only told us part of the story. One of the most famous is by an artist named Warner Sallman. In this one, Jesus is bearded, white, and looking off in the distance, neither stoic nor emotional, just serene. That painting doesn't tell us the whole story.

Even those other popular images of Jesus welcoming the little children, which of course He did, or rescuing lost sheep, which He also did, don't tell the whole story because He wasn't white, nor was He just nice.

He also wept, He also laughed, and He also got angry.

He had emotions, just like we do.

He was sometimes sad, just as we are.

He often laughed, just like we do.

He sometimes got angry, just like we do.

The difference, though, between Him and us is in how He expressed His emotions. That's something we don't all know how to do in a healthy way, even though Mr. Rogers tried to teach us. During this pandemic, I've become even more of a fan of Mr. Rogers. I have my own red sweater and a Mr. Rogers coffee mug, plus I read his biography and saw two movies about him, but a while ago, I came across a video where Mr. Rogers walks towards the camera, and he says, "I'm angry."

Of course, he doesn't look angry.

I've said it before: it's hard to look angry in a cardigan.

Then he starts singing,

What do you do with the mad that you feel

When you feel so mad you could bite?

When the whole wide world seems oh, so wrong…

And nothing you do seems very right?

I can relate to that song, and maybe you can, too, because we all get mad, but what do we do with the mad that we feel? What did Jesus do with the mad that He felt? We read from the Gospel of John that Jesus told those who were selling the doves, "Take these things out of here! Stop making my Father's house a marketplace!"

We see here that Jesus felt the same anger that we feel, but He did something different with it. First of all, He can say what He's angry about.

Not everyone I know can do that.

In fact, I know a whole lot of people who won't even admit that they're angry.

I'm one of them.

It's hard for me to say that I'm angry because I think I'm always supposed to be nice.

When I was a kid, my parents would ask me, "Joe, what's wrong?" I'd tell them, "Nothing." These days, Sara will ask me, "What are you so mad about?" and I'll say, "I'm mad about you always asking me if I'm mad."

That's not true, of course, but that's what I say because just that simple thing, saying what I'm angry about, is hard for me to do, and I'm not alone, so let me say that in taking a lesson from Jesus, we first have to accept the reality that being angry is a part of being human. Then we have to come to terms with the truth that sometimes our anger is telling us something important that can't be ignored.

Anger isn't always so unreasonable.

Most of the time, we are justified in our anger, but we get all messed up in coming to terms with what it is that we're really angry about, and then deciding what it is that we're going to do about it. The most wonderful detail in our Gospel lesson for today is there in verse 15: "Making a whip of cords, he drove all of them out of the temple, both the sheep and the cattle." In all four of the Gospel accounts of Jesus' life and ministry, He storms into the Temple kicking over tables, scattering the coins of the money changers, and setting free the animals, but only in John does He first make a whip of cords.

Do you know how long it takes to braid a whip of cords?

I don't.

I don't know, not only because I've never done it, but also because when I get angry, I don't stop to do anything that might help me calm down or process my thoughts. Instead, I either just start talking without thinking or go silent and brooding. Hardly, if ever, do I stop what I'm doing to sit down to think about why it is that I'm angry and what it is that I'm going to do about it. Jesus is different.

Jesus gets angry, and then He braids a whip of cords.

Do you know how countercultural that is?

There's an old cartoon I remember where the boss yells at Dad in the office. Then Dad comes home and yells at Mom in the kitchen. Mom goes upstairs to yell at their son, who then walks out into the yard to kick the dog.

Anger.

It can destroy a family like a virus that gets passed on from one to the next.

Another thing we do with anger is keep it inside so that it rots our guts and hollows our spirit. Some try to drown it with liquor, numb it with drugs, either of which is destructive, and few take the time to sit down and really think about it. What am I mad about? Then, what am I going to do about it? The knee jerk response to slam a door, throw a punch, get somebody fired, or lock somebody up so frequently does more harm than good.

Impulsivity isn't the answer, so look to Jesus: We must learn to braid the whip, especially given the year we've all had.

We all have good reason to be angry about something, but we have to stop and listen to our anger for it to do us or our world any good.

A hero of mine was Harris Hines.

He was a member and officer of our church.

He also served on the Georgia Supreme Court as the Chief Justice.

In his farewell address to the judiciary as he prepared for retirement, he reminded those listening how he worked to fight the old "lock him up" order from the bench to get to a better solution and urged those who follow in his footsteps to do the same, for just filling up our prisons is not achieving that higher goal of rehabilitation, even if it feels like it's doing something.

When I've visited prisons and jails, I've seen angry, frustrated people who were put behind bars by angry, frustrated people. That's a lot of misused anger if you ask me, so as a culture, as a nation, we have to learn what to do with anger because it will tear us a part if we misuse it, but you know what it's supposed to do? It's supposed to purify us.

Significant background for understanding what it means for Jesus to storm the Temple is found in the Old Testament book of Malachi. There it's written: "the Lord whom you seek will suddenly come to his temple." And when he gets there, he won't just be nice, walking around shaking hands and kissing babies. No, according to the Prophet Malachi, "He is like a refiner's fire and like fullers' soap; and he will purify the descendants of Levi and refine them like gold and silver, until they present offerings to the Lord in righteousness."

Jesus, fueled by anger, purifies the Temple so that it might no longer be a marketplace, but a Temple.

No longer a den of thieves, be a sanctuary for the hurting.

No longer a place where money is exchanged, and debts are paid, but a place where debts are forgiven.

Now, how did he do it?

Through anger.

Through an anger that is frustrated with what is and directed towards that which stands in the way of a better future.

Our world could use that kind of anger.

Our nation could use that kind of anger.

Even our church could use that kind of anger.

In just a couple of hours, we'll be ordaining and installing a group of new church officers on a big, church *Zoom* call, but before they're ordained and installed, we'll ask them a series of questions. One of my favorites is this: "Will you seek to the serve the people with energy, intelligence, imagination, and love?"

Now, you can imagine using these good things to serve the church, but I tell you this, we also need their frustration because we are not yet the best church we could be, so do not grow satisfied with who we are today.

We also need their irritation.

Patience is good, but too much patience enables us to comfortably settle in where we are.

We need their anger because there is so much wrong in this world that we just cannot be OK with any longer.

It's time to listen to our anger.

It's time to listen to that feeling we feel when we see abuse and consider all the ways people are not valued, are looked over, and are made to feel like they're less than human because of the color of their skin, whom they love, or where they come from.

In order to value all God's people, we have to kick over the structures that maintain things as they are.

Now, I'm not talking about recklessness.

We're a church, not a mob, so we must learn from Christ to braid the whip. We must be bold to do as the Savior taught, to slow down and listen to what your anger is telling you. Stop and listen it, for even through anger, the Spirit may be speaking, calling us away from the ways of death that we have grown used to, and towards new life.

Amen.

Step Into the Light
Numbers 21: 4-9 and John 3: 1-21
Preached on March 14, 2021

There are some figures in Scripture that I find it so easy to relate to. I hope that's true for you because the heroes of our faith, especially when we can see ourselves in their shoes, help to make Scripture and the journey of faith come alive.

For example, when we think about Peter and walking out onto the water, I can just about feel myself sinking because I know what it is to take that first brave step and then to become immediately terrified.

When we hear about Thomas wrestling with his doubts, I think about every question I've ever had but was too afraid to ask.

Dropping off our girls at their first day of school, I was so glad not to be Moses's mother. Still, there was a feeling of helplessness as they walked away from me and into their new classrooms, and my prayer was probably much like hers, that God would watch over them as they left me standing there, knowing that I couldn't be right beside them.

At different times of my life, I've felt something like all of them, even the villains like Pilate or Pharaoh. However, it's hard for me to think about Nicodemus because I know just a little too well what it's like to be in his shoes. He's just a little too familiar, a little too much like me, or I'm a little too much like him, and this struggle of his is my own struggle.

Maybe it's yours, too.

Do you know what it's like to only feel the freedom to admit that you need something when you're sure that no one else is listening?

Do you know what it's like to not have anyone else to talk to about your struggles?

Do you know what it's like to feel the pressure of presenting yourself as whole, self-sufficient, strong, impenetrable, and flawless in the light of day, while falling asleep every night exhausted from pretending that you have it all together when you know you don't?

That's Nicodemus.

This Scripture lesson from the Gospel of John comes around every year, and I dread it because in dealing with him, I have to deal with me. I have to look again into my own heart, and it's hard because every preacher thinks he's supposed to be perfect while knowing that he isn't. Every father feels insufficient underneath his suit of armor. Every husband wants to provide more for his wife and must struggle to believe that his spouse could really love him for who he is. Not a single one of us wants to live in a glass house because there are insecurities that we want to keep hidden from the neighbors who are watching and judging us.

So, at night, Nicodemus goes. You know why.

He goes at night to see Jesus because he can't show the world that he needs a Savior.

In the day, he can't appear to need a single thing, so there is some security in the darkness that enables him to be vulnerable. He can only reveal his need when he won't be seen. It was at night that he said, "Rabbi, we know that you are a teacher who has come from God; for no one can do these signs that you do apart from the presence of God."

Another way to say the same thing is like this: "Rabbi, you can do what I can't."

Do you know how hard it is for some people to say something like that?

Do you know how hard it is for a grown man to say something like that?

Do you know how hard it is for a working mother trying to juggle raising kids and a career to admit to the world how impossible her life feels?

It's hard for every person who is like Nicodemus.

It's hard for all of us who are supposed to know where we are going to stop and ask for directions.

It's hard for all of us who are used to helping people to ask for a little help for ourselves.

When you think you're the one who's supposed to know everything, you think you can't be seen asking too many questions. There's a great Jerry Clower story that Nicodemus kind of reminds me of. It's called *The Chauffeur and the Professor*. Now, brother Clower can tell it better than I ever could. I encourage you to listen to his version as soon as possible. The gist of the story is that a genius-level professor has been going around the nation making an incredible speech with the same chauffeur listening the whole time. The chauffeur tells him that he's memorized the professor's speech and can probably make that speech better than the Great PhD ever could, even though he hasn't graduated from the great school of minds. He's an unlettered chauffeur, but he's sure he can make that speech. The Professor, wanting to put this too-big-for-his-britches chauffeur back in his place, agrees to let him try. They swap clothes on the way to the next venue, so before this huge university audience is the chauffeur wearing the professor's clothes, and the professor is in the back wearing the chauffeur's clothes.

Brother Clower goes on to say that the chauffeur made that speech. In fact, in Clower's words, "He forever shelled down the corn. He shelled the corn all the way to the cobb." Translation: he made the speech really well. The crowd, so amazed, "throwed" their books on the floor, screamed in jubilation, gave him a standing ovation. Once they had been calmed down, the university president invited the crowd, if they would like, to ask any questions.

Now, that meant trouble.

The chauffer had the speech memorized, but hadn't thought about the Q and A. A very intelligent young man lifted his hand and asked the most detailed question you've ever heard. Something about carbon dating, stratospheres, and the layers of the earth's crust. The chauffer dressed up like a professor listened to the question. You would imagine that he was sweating, but he kept his cool, took off his glasses like this and said, "Young man, as long as I've been giving this speech throughout North America's most prestigious universities, that's about the simplest question I've ever heard. I'm surprised this university let in someone who would ask a question that simple. In fact, it's so simple, I'll just ask my chauffeur to stand up here and answer it."

Now this story is funny because the professor is wearing the chauffeur's clothes, but the truth is that, to some degree or another, the professor always feels like a chauffeur in professor's clothes. The truth is that, to some degree or another, the preacher always feels like a sinner in preacher's clothes. The truth is that, to some degree or another, we all feel like imposters, fakers, travelers, just on the way to perfection, while the world seems to want us to have made it there already. Who among us is truly a self-made man?

Who among us is self-sufficient?

Who among us knows what he's doing and has it all together?

We point our fingers at entitlement in the world, while knowing that we all depend on so much help that just the idea that we're doing fine on our own is a mirage. Knowing that he must keep such an image, such a mirage, intact, Nicodemus goes to see Jesus at night.

You know why.

It's because the world wants to put him up on a pedestal that he would love to come down from. It's because the act that he's keeping up is wearing him down, but he can't get off the hamster wheel.

It's because he needs help but is afraid to ask for it, and so he goes to see the Savior at night, and this is what the Savior says: "You have to be born again."

Nicodemus asks, "How can anyone be born after having grown old? Can one enter a second time into his mother's womb and be born?"

What's going on here is Nicodemus is resisting the idea of starting over.

He's resisting the thought of being as helpless as a newborn.

Having made it this far, how can I begin again?

Having built up so much respect, how could I bow in need before this Jesus from Galilee?

It's as though he's asking, "I've built up a life for myself, and you want me to give it away?"

The answer is, "yes."

We see it again and again.

The rich young ruler must walk away from the life he has to gain eternal life. Later in John's Gospel, Jesus will say, "Those who love their life will lose it, and those who hate their life in this world will keep it for eternal life." What does all that mean? It means that if you're so afraid of losing what you have that you won't admit that you need some help, you're going to lose it anyway.

It means that if you're so consumed with appearing perfect to this world that you won't ever show vulnerability, then your dirty laundry will expose you sooner or later. It means that people like Nicodemus, people like us, may as well risk being a little more real than we have been because that's the only way we're ever going to get right.

In our really strange Old Testament lesson with all the snakes, we heard how people were hiding in the shadows with their snake bites, but in order to be healed, they had to come out into the light of day, revealing their wounds.

Doesn't that sound like a good word for us today?

For us, who present to the world a polished image that says, "We're doing just fine," though really, we're drowning in debt, our kids drive us crazy, and we sure could use some help. Guess what: we're never going to get any until we're willing to cry out for it.

We're never going to be saved until we admit that we need to be saved.

We'll never be able to be found until we admit that we're lost.

We are covered up in shadow, so step into the light.

Step into the light instead.

In the light, there is no condemnation, but only healing.

In Christ is life and not death. Show Him your wounds and find healing.

Confess to Him your sins and receive forgiveness.

Kneel before the Savior of the world and live.

Amen.

Reverent Submission
Hebrews 5: 5-10 and John 12: 20-36
Preached on March 21, 2021

On more than one occasion, I've made fun of the great early 20th Century governor of Texas Miriam A. Ferguson. Though she was the second female governor in United States history, the first female governor of the great state of Texas, a college graduate, and was, by most accounts, a great leader, a populist, a fiscal conservative, and a great opponent of the Ku Klux Klan, she is perhaps most famous for saying, "If English was good enough for Jesus, it's good enough for Texas schoolchildren."

Jesus, you see, did not speak English.

He spoke a language called Aramaic, but seminary students, trained to read Scripture, in the language Scripture was first uttered in, learn to read, not Aramaic, but Hebrew and Greek. I knew why I was supposed to learn Hebrew, however, on my first day of Greek class when I first started seminary, I had no idea why we were being forced to learn Greek, and I couldn't figure out why we weren't learning Aramaic. I was too embarrassed to ask anyone why we were learning Greek, so I just went on learning it, not knowing why I was learning it, until one day I overheard a conversation on the subject: "Greek was the universal written language of Jesus' world," so the Gospels were not written in Aramaic, as it was not much of a written language, not Hebrew, as pretty much only Jews learned to read that, but Greek, which was at the time the language of pretty much everyone.

It was the language of Asia Minor, Ethiopia, and Spain.

It was, at the time of Jesus, the written language of the Roman Empire.

At that time, Greek was what Latin was to the world for much of the Common Era during the great expansions of the Roman Catholic Church, and what English is to much of the world today. In language schools in Tokyo and Paris, children learn English because their parents want to give them a leg up. Bands from Germany, Afghanistan, and Singapore sing in English to appeal to a wider audience. English might be the closest thing the world has today to a universal written language. It is the language of the most powerful nation on earth. It is the language used in the most exciting movies anyone can see. It is the language of President Joe Biden, William Shakespeare, and Wall Street. People who have something to say to the world today are saying it in English, just as people who had something that was worth saying in the ancient world wrote it in Greek. It was the language that people who were educated enough to be literate learned to read; it was the language of Homer, the language of democracy, power, empire, and influence.

So these Greeks go to Philip.

We assume that something about living in Bethsaida in Galilee meant that he could understand their Greek or that they all could speak Hebrew, regardless, these Greeks go to Philip in the hope of seeing Jesus but it's important to think about why.

Why would these Greeks go to see Jesus?

Not only was their language the one that everyone spoke, but also what did the Greeks need from anyone else?

Athens was the peak of culture and wisdom at the time and is still one that many societies hope to emulate, so what did these Greeks need from Jesus?

These Greeks didn't need Jesus the teacher. They were Greek and they already had the greatest philosophers of the time. As we still learn from them today, you might argue that these Greeks had the best philosophers of any time. They had Socrates, Aristotle, Plato, and Diogenes. They had the philosophy of the Stoics, so you can't imagine they needed Rabbi Jesus to teach them.

Not only that, these Greeks had Hippocrates and the most modern medicine available to help them avoid suffering, illness, and disease. Did they need Jesus, the Healer and Miracle Worker? Nor did these Greeks need Jesus the Prince of Peace, as they already had democracy, they trusted the voice of the people, and through election were able to avoid the tyranny of leaders too powerful.

I believe that we can safely assume that they didn't need any of the things that people often go to Jesus looking for, so we should wonder why they went up saying, "Sir, we wish to see Jesus." What did the Greeks need with any other culture?

Why did they want to see Jesus?

It would be like a French chef from the Le Cordon Bleu traveling to New York City to learn how to cook.

It would be like our NASA calling up the Soviet Union in the heat of space race, asking for a little help getting a rocket off the ground.

The great cultures of the world don't go across boarders asking for help. It's hard for me to imagine even people from regions of the same country asking for help from their fellow countrymen.

Last week, I was thinking about the TV show *Hee Haw*. One episode had Grandpa announcing to his family, "Well everyone, I'm moving up north." The family couldn't believe it. "Why, Grandpa, would you ever do something like that. You don't even like people from up there. You call them Yankees and complain about them all the time." "Well, family," Grandpa says, "I'm getting up there in years, and I figure it's better for one of them to die than one of us."

There it is.

Would Grandpa go up north asking for help? Never! Notice, though, not the South nor the North, not the Greeks nor the Romans, has figured out what do with death.

Certainly, we don't have it figured out.

I'm reminded of that every time I hear the number of COVID-19 deaths.

Last time I looked it was 535,997 in the U.S. It's a number so large that I had to go and look it up because we don't really put it in the headlines. It's more than half of Cobb County. That's almost nine times the population of Marietta. Itmakes a number like 2,977, the number of people who died on September 11th, or 2,403, the number of U.S. troops killed at Pearl Harbor, look like a drop in the bucket.

It's more than we lost in World War I.

It's more than we lost in World War II.

It's more than we lost in Vietnam.

It's more than we lost in all those wars combined.

We can't talk about it, though.

It may be because to lose one is so much to bear.

We're talking about grandmothers, grandfathers, aunts, uncles, mothers, fathers, husbands, and wives. We're talking about people who are gone, some without a funeral; others, who breathed their last without a hand to hold. This is one of the great struggles for all of humanity in all of human history: not just how to live, but how to deal with the reality of death, a reality that every facet of our culture wants to avoid.

When they go to see Jesus, He offers them something that no other culture, not Greek culture and not our culture, could have offered. When the Greeks want to see Jesus, He gives them this: *Unless a grain of wheat falls into the earth and dies, it remains just a single grain; but if it dies it bears much fruit.*

He gives them a reverent submission to the reality of death rather than an urgent denial or even a miracle cure. "Now my soul is troubled [He said]. And what should I say, 'Father, save me from this hour'? No, it is for this reason that I have come to this hour. Father, glorify your name."

You see, the way of Christ is not the way of our culture, as Christ does not fear death. In fact, he submits to it. He doesn't run away from it. He looks it in the eye, for in every needless death is a lesson to learn and in every sacrifice is the seed of new life.

Like these Greeks, we, too, must learn from this teaching, for as we look over this earth as the champions of the Space Race and the greatest military power the world has ever seen, we are slow to face the glaring frailty that half a million deaths reveal.

Yet, might each one be a seed that pushes us to create a more noble healthcare system?

Might each one be a seed planted that sprouts in us a desire to eliminate misinformation, for propaganda and denial cost human lives?

Furthermore, as this virus has spread the world over, person to person and place to place, we are invited to see that our borders hardly mean anything. There is no wall we could build that a virus would not pass through, and so let us hear from the Prince of Peace, let us hear it in the deaths of so many sisters and brothers the world over, that Christ invites us to share more than an infection, Christ invites us to reach across the boundary lines, the rivers, the fences, and the lawns to create a better world, better neighborhoods, better communities, a better future, by learning the lessons that death has to teach.

Today, as we struggle to understand how eight people were murdered, six of them Asian Americans, let us recognize that the way we talk, the way we see people, and that just calling something the "China Virus," can have divisive and dehumanizing effects.

In death, there is a lesson for us to learn, and despite everything that we have, everything we've done, and this great nation that we've built, we've been dealing in hatred and division for too long, so let us learn now what death has to teach.

Consider Rome, who took our Jesus and nailed Him to a cross, trying to preserve power and maintain the order of the way things had been.

His blood changed everything.

His sacrifice changed everything because death has its own enlightenment to offer us.

Let us embody enough humility and reverent submission to learn.

Amen.

He Entered Jerusalem
Psalm 118: 1-2, 19-29, and Mark 11: 1-11

Preached on March 28, 2021

For the last five weeks, Rev. Cassie Waits and I have had the honor of talking with experts in different fields to learn more about how to practice our faith. To learn about observing the Sabbath, we talked with two people, one Protestant woman who just started really resting on the Sabbath and one Jewish woman who grew up doing it. Then, thinking about singing, last Wednesday we talked with two who have each dedicated their lives to music. To learn about how to celebrate our bodies as temples where the Holy Spirit resides, we talked with a fitness instructor and an ER doc. Each week, we, two of your pastors, took the seat of student to learn about things we don't know a whole lot about, and each Wednesday, Cassie assigned homework so that we all might practice doing these things we haven't mastered and maybe get a little bit better at them.

That's what practice is for.

You haven't mastered it, so you try it and get better and better.

I remember baseball practice.

At the apex of my baseball career, I was sitting the bench for the Marietta High School Blue Devils, but five or six days a week we practiced, and I took that practice seriously. Why? It's because at any moment, Coach might send me into the game. That's how it is with so many of us who practice at different things. Choirs practice and practice, and then they sing. Some people practice their French in private but then take a big trip. On the day the plane lands in Paris, maybe they're still not masters, but there is a difference between practicing something at home and doing it out in the open where people can hear and see you.

What I want to point out to you this morning is that we have to practice our faith to get better because, on the one hand, following Jesus is just like anything else. The more we practice, the better at it we get, but there's also a difference between baseball practice and practicing our faith. The baseball games are scheduled. You know when they're coming up. When it comes to our faith, there's no way of knowing when practice is over and the game has begun. You just have to practice and practice for that moment, knowing that you might need the honed skills of a Christian at the drop of a hat.

Scripture says these moments come like a thief in the night. Thieves don't call a week ahead to let you know that they'll be stopping by. Likewise, we don't know when that moment will be that we'll need to know how to pray, but we do know that the moment is coming.

I remember so vividly this moment just before our oldest daughter was born. We didn't know it, but the cord was wrapped around her neck, and during delivery, all at once, her heartbeat slowed. You can imagine what this was like. We went from anticipation to dealing in matters of life and death. Out of nowhere, my wife Sara was being pulled from the room and into surgery. Her bed went down the hall and I wasn't allowed to go with her. I said to my mother-in-law, "What do I do?" and she said, "Joe, this is when we pray."

You see, we practice our faith because we don't know when the big game is scheduled.

We practice our faith, and when the moment comes, either we're ready or we're not.

Either we know what to do or we don't.

Jesus was ready, and this is His moment.

For so long, He'd been telling anyone who would listen: "I must go to Jerusalem to die. That's what I came here to do. These sinful people don't understand anything. They have confused love and power, faith and laws, so I'm going to Jerusalem, and maybe if they crucify me, they'll finally see that they have this whole thing turned upside down." That's what Palm Sunday is all about, you see. He'd been practicing, and it hadn't been easy for Him.

Do you remember how He told Peter that He has to go to Jerusalem to die?

It was when they went up on top of the mountain, and not only did Peter try to get them to stay up on top of the mountaintop, but Peter also tried to talk Jesus out of going to Jerusalem. Surely, it wasn't easy for Jesus to say to His friend, "Get behind me, Satan, for you are setting your mind, not on divine things but on human things."

In that moment, Christ set His sights on Jerusalem.

Likely, He had been preparing Himself for it long before then, but today is game day.

Today, the plane has landed, and He's getting off whether He's ready or not.

The people are cheering, although you can imagine Him weeping because He's been preparing himself, not with rose-tinted glasses, but seeing right through the cheers, knowing that before Him is the cross.

He was ready, and He rode onward.

On the other hand, we know that so many others claimed to follow Him, yet game day came, and they forgot everything.

I've been thinking a lot about the two mass shootings that have happened recently. The editorial cartoon in last Wednesday's paper said, "I guess now we know things really are getting back to normal."

Two mass shootings in one month.

You know as well as I do that this is not normal.

A sobering reality of how out of whack our society is, is how so many of these murderers were raised in church, which leads me to my point: we all need to practice this faith a little bit harder because there are some who take action in this world, who walk out onto the field on gameday and act as though they've never heard the words:

"Love your neighbor as yourself."

"Render to no one evil for evil."

"This is the day that the Lord has made, so let us rejoice and be glad in it."

"Give thanks to the Lord, for He is good; His steadfast love endures forever."

The game came and they forgot everything, or else, they had been practicing hate instead of love, for they denied the Gospel with their actions.

They mistook their brothers and sisters.

They did exactly the opposite of what the One we follow exemplified, and it tears me up inside. It makes me sick to my core, and it makes me want to shout from the mountaintops: "Christians, it's time to practice what we preach."

For what we preach is love.

What we preach is freedom.

What we preach is human dignity, having sung since the nursery that each and every one is precious in His sight.

That's what we must practice.

That's what we must practice until the Father's love spills right out of us.

We need to practice our faith, and let me tell you what happens when we do. A couple weeks ago, Rev. Joe Brice and Katherine Harrison were talking with Cassie and me about our book. The chapter was about saying "yes" and saying "no," and Joe walked us through a series of statements trying to prove to us how easy it can be to say "no" if we just practice.

He says, "Repeat after me: the light is on."

You see, you can just say that. It's easy to say. The light is on.

"The wall is green," he said next, and we said that.

Then, "I don't have time to do that as well as I would like," which we all repeated, though it was a little difficult because we don't all often say it.

The purpose of the exercise was to prove that the more you practice saying something, the easier it is to say it, and I tell you all this so that you'll know why what I'm about to tell you matters. Last Tuesday was Bud Tubb's funeral, but Dr. Jim Speed said to the family as soon as he saw them, "This is a good day," and he said it, not as forced words, not as empty words, not as hopeful words, but as a matter of fact. He said it just as plain as if he had just said the light is on or the wall is green because when people practice their faith, it's there when they need it; and having practiced His faith since the day He was born, Jesus Christ rode into Jerusalem knowing what He was in for, ready for what awaited, that you and I might face death without fear. Because He practiced what He preached and did what He knew was right, because He rode into Jerusalem though He knew death awaited him, today we may know full well that those who die in the Lord are not lost. Instead, we trust that they are going home.

Let us practice our faith so that like them, we know the way there.

Amen.

Let Us Be Glad and Rejoice in His Salvation
Isaiah 25: 6-9 and John 20: 1-18
Preached on April 4, 2021

Sometimes, people ask me about my Easter Sunday sermon. In the last week or so, a few friends have asked, "Joe, big Sunday coming up. What are you going to preach on?"

"Well, I've been thinking about a sermon on the resurrection," I've responded.

In a lot of ways, it's easy to preach on Easter Sunday.

It's all right here.

Today is the day.

There's not much left for the preacher to explain or illustrate.

He is risen. He is risen indeed. Thanks be to God. What more need be said? Yet this is what I want to emphasize today: that what happened on Easter Sunday so long ago, when Mary went looking for a corpse to bury and instead encountered the Lord, risen from the dead, changes everything.

It doesn't just change the way we look at death, no longer with fear but hope for our own life eternal, but it must change the way we look at the everyday, from the moment we rise up in the morning to when we put our heads down on our pillows at night. From the moment we sit down at our desks, bored already, or walk through the front door, not at all enthused about getting to another baseball practice. The resurrection must change our perspective on all the good plans that fall apart and all the crushing blows that have us reeling because the truth of the resurrection colors how we understand the world around us and changes the way we understand what happens to us from our greatest successes to our deepest disappointments.

Faith changes things.

Faith in the resurrection changes things.

Now, if you asked me to define a word like *faith*, I'd say something like what I just said, that faith is a way of looking at the world and understanding our lives so that we never fall victim to despair and avoid getting lost in temptation or heartache. Faith is like a lot of the words Christians like us use, only when we are asked to define them, we struggle to do so simply. When I'm searching for a good way to define one of our Christian code words,

I often look them up in a short dictionary written by one of my favorite preachers, Frederick Buechner. When he defines the word faith, he quotes the book of Hebrews, "Faith is the assurance of things hoped for, the conviction of things not seen."

Then, referring to Sarah, whom God told would have a child in her old age, Buechner says that "Faith is laughter at the promise of a child… [and] Faith dies, as it lives, laughing. Faith is better understood as a verb than as a noun, as a process than as a possession… Faith is not being sure where you're going but going anyway." Buechner goes on to compare faith to friendship, which, should you put it to the test, you'd ruin it. Ask someone to prove that she's really your friend and watch how it hurts her. Likewise, faith can't be proven but that hardly means it isn't true.

A life of faith is one lived expecting something good to happen because you know good things have happened before, and it enables us, not just to look in one empty tomb but every empty tomb with the hope of people who are willing to be surprised by God despite a mountain of disappointment.

What I'm trying to say here isn't something simple, but of course it is.

Simply put, faith is just a way of looking at the world and filling in what you don't know, and so while we Christians often strictly define faith in positive terms, it also takes faith to look out on the unformed future with pessimism because no one knows that they'll be disappointed, while people often walk around with the faith that they will be.

You see, people who are always pessimistic don't know it all.

They don't expect surprises, though surprises come.

Have you ever met someone who said, "I'm not a pessimist, I'm just realistic?"

That's not entirely true, for it's not realistic to never expect anything good to ever happen. Good things happen all the time. For example, Mary was being pessimistic and realistic when she looked into the tomb, but it was empty.

The prophet Ezekiel went to a valley of dry bones, and they all came back to life.

The Hebrew people were saved from slavery in Egypt.

David slayed a giant with a rock and a sling, and the pessimist would have bet against him in that fight and would have lost it all because the giant fell.

Christian faith calls us to take surprises into account, and real life often surprises us just as the old Bible stories do. Think about it. You can imagine how many people told Orville and Wilbur Wright that their plane would never get off the ground? Likewise, I once told my daughter that she could keep the old dryer I put on the side of the road if she pushed it up a hill. I told her that with pessimistic faith that she'd never be able to do it, and yet she did. I was even more surprised by her than I was at a ball I once attended in Columbia, Tennessee wearing just most of a tuxedo. No one even made fun of me for my lack of cummerbund, though I expected someone to.

I tell you that because only a fool is always pessimistic.

A fool goes through life imagining everything is going to turn out badly.

A fool confuses pessimism with realism.

Murphy's Law discounts the hand of God.

Lacking optimistic, hopeful imagination is a sorry way to go through life, for miracles spring up all around us, and I don't want you to miss them.

Consider faith then, the kind of faith that the resurrection inspires, which is nothing more than taking what you know God has done and daring to believe that God might do it again.

Faith is seeing a church, wounded by division and decline and imagining that it might be named the Best Place to Worship in Cobb County three years in a row.

Faith is planting seeds in the ground and expecting them to grow.

Faith is sending kids to school and trusting that they'll learn.

Faith is driving your car into a roundabout and daring to believe that you'll survive.

Faith is taking the truth of an empty tomb and allowing it to color your vision of every relationship that feels like it's hit a brick wall, for how many times has reconciliation happened?

How many times have you said, "I bet she'll never call," and then the phone rang?

How many days have you been sure that nothing would ever change, and yet it did?

How many mornings felt like Groundhog Day, and yet a new day dawned.

I tell you; it's happened plenty of times. It's happened far too often for you or me to have the outlook of a pessimist.

Easter Sunday calls on us to take the truth of the resurrection and allow it to change the way we see the world around us. It is a day for celebrating every seed that bloomed into flower though it seemed to be nothing more than a seed; every child sent off to college who came back educated and purpose-filled. Today is the day for giving thanks to God that even this season of pandemic is ending, and now we have the chance to do things differently than we did before because it did not end us or close the book on our story.

My friends, we can write a new story starting now.

We can write it with greater kindness,

Greater unity,

More respect,

And common decency.

Having seen poverty and felt disease this last year, we may now dare to believe that something might be done to ensure a brighter future. Having heard the people shout for justice, we might listen and reimagine rather than get stuck in the cycle of the way things are.

On this Resurrection Day, dare to believe that new life is jumping up from the ground and leaping from every tomb, for there is no power in death other than the power that we give it. Christ has conquered it, and it is not the end.

Today is the beginning.

For He has risen. He has risen indeed.

Let us be glad and rejoice in His salvation.

Amen.

Why Are You Frightened?
1 John 3: 1-7 and Luke 24: 36b-48

Preached on April 14, 2021

I've always been scared of ghosts.

Seriously.

Since I was little, I've been scared of ghosts, even more than snakes or heights or anything else.

I remember being young, like six or seven, in my grandmother's basement with my older cousins, who thought it would be fun to play with an old Ouija board we found. Do you know those things, with the mystical planchette that you use to communicate with the dead? It probably was fun playing with that thing for the first few minutes as my cousins summoned the spirits of our dead relatives, until I screamed so loud that my grandmother heard me, ran downstairs, and they all got in big trouble.

I'm not sure exactly what it is with ghosts, but there is something about them that unsettles me, which is true for a lot of people. Many people are scared of ghosts. If they weren't, no one would scream in scary movies, and they do scream in scary movies. I've been one of them.

What we know from every horror film that has ever been made is that ghosts rarely come visit people to tell funny jokes or make them feel better. Ghosts appear to scare people in the movies, sometimes to warn them like they did Ebenezer Scrooge in *A Christmas Carol*, or to let the living know that their souls will never be at rest unless they are avenged like they do in so many Shakespeare plays, so if a ghost shows up, literature, movies, and experience have taught us to be afraid.

The disciples were too.

What's clear from our second Scripture lesson is that they thought He was a ghost.

That sounds strange to our ears. Just the idea that they would have been scared of our gentle Savior sounds very strange, but they were. They were "terrified," Luke's Gospel tells us.

Why?

Why did they scream like little kids or a grown pastor in a horror movie?

Why weren't they excited?

Why weren't they relieved?

Think about it with me this way: had Shakespeare been the one to write the Gospel of Luke, I imagine he might have made Jesus something like the ghost King of Denmark in *Hamlet*. Maybe Jesus would have showed up as a ghost to tell the disciples who is to blame for His death just as the ghost king tells his son, Hamlet, to avenge his murder by killing the new king, Hamlet's uncle; only worse, if this were the case, then the ghost, seeking revenge, showed up to haunt the very ones who were partly guilty for his death.

Certainly, if Jesus were a ghost, then He showed up to haunt the ones who felt guilty for His death. Surely, they had spent their time hiding in that locked room feeling shame.

They were thinking about how only the women were with Him in the end.

They were thinking about how they were the ones He called brothers, yet they abandoned, betrayed, or denied Him, and maybe they were thinking that now His soul will never rest until justice is paid in full.

That's what ghosts show up to do in the popular imagination, dredge up the past, and so the Gospel of Luke tells us that, "Jesus himself stood among them and said to them,

Peace be with you. [Despite this peaceful greeting,] they were startled and terrified and thought they were seeing a ghost. Jesus said to them, "Why are you frightened...?"

I can pretty easily answer that question, and I bet you can, too.

Had it been me standing there, I would have assumed that Jesus' ghost had returned to let me know how disappointed He was in me for failing Him in that crucial moment.

He would have spoken of that moment that led to an innocent man's death, and how I wasn't brave enough to do anything about it or to at least die up there with Him.

Isn't that what we all assume ghosts are all about?

Can you think of a single ghost who comes back from the dead to let his friends and family know how proud he is of all of them?

Think about the ghosts you've heard about.

The Headless Horseman wants a new head.

The creepy twins in *The Shining* want someone to come and play, which is a mundane invitation that only a ghost can make sound terrifying.

Little Cole Sear "sees dead people" in *The Sixth Sense*, and why? Why do the dead appear to him? From *Macbeth*, Shakespeare gives us his answer:

And oftentimes, to win us to our harm
The instruments of darkness tell us truths
Win us with honest trifles and betrayals
Of deepest consequence.

What do the disciples assume Jesus wants?

Judas was dead already, but Peter still lived.

Had Jesus returned to hold him to account for what he'd done or failed to do?

When we think of ghosts, that's something of what we think of. Even Casper the Friendly Ghost wants help making peace with his past, so if the disciples are afraid, we might assume they thought He was a ghost who had come back to haunt them, how my grandmother once threatened my mom: "Cathy, when I die, and you clean out my house, if you pull all my things out front for a yard sale, I'll haunt you for the rest of your life."

That's how we think.

We imagine that souls will return to earth to let us know how we've failed them.

We have nightmares of our beloved whispering one last word, one last message.

We long for their words to be loving or affirming, but we fear they're disappointed in us.

We return to the tomb of fathers and grandfathers worried that we haven't lived up to the calling. Some even imagine that one day they will have to stand before Almighty God, and when their deeds are weighed, He will either be pleased or disappointed.

My friends, if you imagine that Christ would show up like a ghost who is disappointed in you then you have forgotten Who He is. Just as Christ asked the disciples, we must ask ourselves, "Why are you frightened, and why do doubts arise in your hearts?" for Christ is not a ghost, and vengeance is not what He's looking for. Christ comes to them alive, and He comes now just as He lived: full of love and forgiveness, consistent with Who He always said He would be.

He's not like the Headless Horseman searching to do more harm in death as he'd done in life, but like the father who welcomes the Prodigal Son home.

He's not like any of the figures of horror movies who terrorize the living, but like Esau, who offers his brother Jacob the kind of forgiveness that he did not deserve.

He's not like the Ghost of Christmas Yet to Come, who showed Scrooge his grave by pointing towards it with a shrouded bone of a finger, but like the Lamb of God Most Holy, Who invites us through the gates of Heaven by opening His arms wide to embrace us fully.

We all forget, even disciples forget, what God is like sometimes, and we think that He blames us for getting lost, when all He really wants is to find us again.

I recently read a sermon by the great Howard Thurman. Thurman is now considered the brilliant theological mind of the Civil Rights Movement. He was from Florida and wrote and preached all over, teaching religion at Morehouse and Howard, traveling to India to meet with Gandhi, and when thinking about the parable of the lost coin and the lost sheep, he imagines what it might be like to find yourself as a lost sheep:

A sheep was enjoying his grass and the other things that sheep enjoy as he went along, and then when he started feeling chilly, he didn't recall, but the only thing that he remembers is that suddenly he became aware that he was cold, and there was a throwback in his mind, and he realized that he had been cold for some time. But the grass was good. Then he looked around and he discovered that he was alone. That everybody had gone. That is, that all the sheep had gone. And he began crying aloud. And then the shepherd, who had many sheep, missed him when he got back to the fold, and he left his ninety and nine – or whatever the number was – and he went out to try to find this sheep that was lost. And Jesus said, "God is like that."

Well of course He is, but when we find ourselves all alone, for some reason it becomes easier to believe in ghosts than in the loving, merciful Shepherd, so hear this: imagining that Peter and the others are afraid, He does what Jesus always does. Jesus, seeking out what is precious and lost, finds them and rejoices. He greets them not with anger, but with joy; not with blame, but thanksgiving. He's not mad at Peter; He just wants His friend to come back to the fold.

That is what we must remember today.

As Rev. Cassie Waits so beautifully put it in her sermon last Sunday, for a year now, we've been like these disciples, locked behind closed doors, and now we must get back out again. The problem is that to leave, we first must conquer our fear of ghosts because lockdown started, and then it lasted.

No one has had dinner together.

No one has seen you.

How, then, do you start again after not speaking for a year?

There are likely all kinds of thoughts in your minds. The kind of thoughts that wake us up at night: what if they don't like me anymore? What if they're disappointed? What if they're mad at me? These are the kinds of thoughts that lurk in our imaginations and keep us confined to self-imposed prisons, so the Savior walks right in and shows us how it's done.

It all starts just by Him asking, "Have you anything here to eat?"

There is the traditional way to explain this request: ghosts don't eat. By asking for food, Jesus shows the disciples that He's a living man resurrected from the dead; however, there's something else to this request, for in making it, Jesus shows us that reconciliation is only as complicated as we let it be.

A chasm can be bridged over a simple meal.

The difference between a ghost and a real person is that ghosts aren't real, so don't let your fear of them keep you from living abundantly. All you have to do is show up on a doorstep, trusting that death never has the final word when the Risen Lord is on our side.

Our first Scripture lesson put it this way: "See what love the father has given us… Beloved, we are God's children now; what we will be has not yet been revealed," so don't assume that you know how the story ends. You still have the chance to come back home to community and fellowship, for Christ welcomes us all, and we must be bold to welcome home each other. This is the reality of the Father's love; how He could have remained in the tomb and allowed our rejection of Him to have the final word, but instead He sought us out again, not as a ghost, but as a loving Father Who wants nothing more than to love His children and to bring them back home. Thanks be to God for His wonderous love.

Now, let us share it with the world, for we are witnesses to these things.

Amen.

From Mother's Day to Pentecost, and the End of a Very Strange School Year

The spring holidays are not always greeted with the same pomp and circumstance as Christmas and Easter, but during this pandemic year it seemed important to talk about these special holidays. In the following sermons, I tried to celebrate well the way that a mother's love is like God's love, why graduating from high school is always worth celebrating, even if it can't be celebrated in the traditional way, and why Pentecost matters in this time when streaming church was embraced by so many.

Savior, Like a Shepherd Lead Us
John 10: 11-18 and 1 John 3: 16-24
Preached on April 25, 2021

The great religions of the world have so much in common, but there are differences of course, which, along with the many similarities, are also important to pay attention to. For example, last Wednesday morning, I was honored to attend a breakfast meeting of local religious leaders hosted by Roswell Street Baptist Church. A new friend of mine, Rabbi Larry Sernovitz of Temple Kol Emeth, was there. As the two of us were talking about the incredible pair of shoes he had on, a woman handed him his breakfast: hash brown casserole and bacon. This was a moment of difference, which was addressed, politely resolved, and would have been foolish to ignore. For us to eat together, we can't ignore the reality that not all foods are kosher, and so we don't all eat the same things.

That's important to think about.

That's how it is.

We can't allow what's different to divide us, but we can't be ignorant of what might offend our friends and neighbors, and there are also moments when what makes us unique is worth celebrating. Think about what all makes us unique and different from Hindus, Sikhs, Buddhists, and Muslims. One unique Christian attribute among many is the image of the shepherd. It is an image of God, a metaphor for understanding the divine that we share with our Jewish brothers and sisters. The image of the shepherd runs throughout today's worship service from the Call to Worship, the Prayer of Confession, first and second Scripture lessons, and all the music that we've heard. This image is most associated with the 23rd Psalm, which belonged to the Jewish faith long before Hobby Lobby ever put it on a wall hanging or a beach towel. You might think I'm kidding about that, but you can get Psalm 23 on a beach towel, though where it really belongs is in our hearts and captured by our minds so that we can recall it when we need it most, for when we walk through the valley of the shadow of death, it is imperative that we remember Who is with us. Whenever a Christian thinks about what it means to know Who God is, it is a comfort to go back to those most wonderful words which Cheryl, Chohee, Will, and Jeffrey put to music so beautifully:

The Lord is my shepherd; I shall not want.

He maketh me to lie down in green pastures; he leadeth me beside the still waters.

He restoreth my soul; he leadeth me in the paths of righteousness for his name's sake. Yea, though I walk through the valley of the shadow of death, I will fear no evil: for thou art with me.

I could go on reading this psalm. It is a sermon in and of itself, but I want to stop right there to point out this defining characteristic of our religion that is there in the last phrase I read: namely that in our faith, to survive, to have salvation, to live, is to be not alone.

Think about it. What is it that comforts the sheep? It is the presence of the shepherd, and what does the shepherd do, especially for those who wander from the fold, who find themselves lost and alone?

The shepherd finds them.

The shepherd walks with them.

The shepherd brings them back into community.

The shepherd restores the isolated into the family of faith.

The shepherd seeks out those who are alone so that they won't be alone any longer.

That's different from some other religions. Being restored into the community is a different goal from what many are steadily working towards, for some are working towards the peace and quiet of solitude rather than the noise and bickering of the Father's House. I'm thinking now of the enlightened mystic who has discovered the secrets to the universe by quieting the mind. I have this image of a hermit guru who sits on top of a mountain, resentful of those who climb up to ask him the meaning of life. In fact, this image was in a political cartoon just this morning in the *Atlanta Journal Constitution*. These figures that we see from time to time in the movies or elsewhere are based on real people, like Vijay Gopala, who recently spent 17 years living in meditative silence in an Indian forest, or the Buddha who sat under a Bodhi tree for 49 days straight. They are the great adherents of Hindu and Buddhist asceticism. We know that such a strain exists in Christianity, and even Christ himself went out to the desert for 40 days and 40 nights, but salvation for us looks a little bit less like the mountaintop guru's enlightenment because for us, we receive the answers we seek once we've made it back to the flock, not when we've removed ourselves from them.

We see this in Scripture.

It's there in both of today's Scripture readings as well as so many others.

In the Bible, there are so many accounts of God's people finding their way back to community, and so there is a son who wanders off, spends his inheritance, and once he's broke and all his fair-weather friends leave him, he tries to make a living slopping the hogs. This is a version of hell in our religion. To be lost, alone, and far from home is the opposite of where God thinks we ought to be, and so to be saved by God is something like what we see in this son's father, who embraces him and restores him into a community.

The same is true of Jonah, who tries to run away but keeps being brought back to people, even people whom he doesn't like very much. Likewise, Moses leaves Egypt but must return to his tribe because that's just how it is. Again, and again, this is the story. Ruth and Naomi find their way to a new homeland and a new community. The lost coin is found, the lost sheep gets back to the flock, the lost son finds his way home. Our God is a Shepherd Who tries to get us back into groups where we'll finally be happy, only think about this for a minute: how many of us think that we'll only really be happy once we've gotten away from everybody?

I have a friend who once told me that he went to visit his father in his new home out west. His dad is retired, divorced, and wealthy, so he left everything and everyone to live on top of a mountain in a cabin overlooking a valley. Apparently, it is the most picturesque prison you've ever seen.

My friends, in which direction is your life headed? Are you moving towards community or away from it?

After 14 months of pandemic functioning, do you even remember how to be around people? That's OK if you don't because all of us are a little awkward right now, but remember this: when it comes to our faith, moving towards others is moving towards salvation while moving away is like walking towards hell.

For this reason, I worry about our culture all the time.

I worry about which religion has really taken our nation over.

The social fabric of our society strains under the weight of deferred maintenance on basic human relationships.

The institutions that once held us together are neglected.

The poor live out of sight from the rich.

The imprisoned are locked behind doors and punished with solitary confinement.

Add on top of that the fear of a virus that still keeps many of us home.

Plus, our response to that same virus divides us between those who wear masks and those who don't. In the midst of all of that, I can't help but think that we have forgotten how to get along. Not only that, we have forgotten what it means to be Christian.

Some people, maybe many people, believe that being a Christian can be reduced down to a few simple standards of belief, and so they'll say that we're no longer a Christian country because we no longer believe all the same things that we used to. However, let us not forget what lies at the core of who we are and Who we know God to be; from the 23rd Psalm to the story of the Prodigal Son, we know that our God is a God of relationship, and that the Divine is present whenever two or more are gathered together.

We must never think that being solid in our convictions but isolated and alone is the picture of one who follows Jesus. To be Christian means to be restored in community, and to work for the restoration of all God's children. We cannot be Christians all by ourselves. It says it right there in our second Scripture lesson:

We know love by this, that he laid down his life for us – and we ought to lay down our lives for one another. How does God's love abide in anyone who has the world's goods and sees a brother or sister in need and yet refuses to help?

That's a good question, and we must not make it too complicated because we don't have to look very far these days to find people who are in need. I imagine you can think of someone who needs what you have to offer just right across the street. Just think about it. There is now a ministry of loneliness in the United Kingdom. The government has organized to do something about what some consider to be a loneliness crisis, believing that being lonely for a day is as bad for your body as smoking 15 cigarettes.

Have you ever thought about that?

Some of your neighbors only leave the house to go to the grocery store.

Some folks on your street walk outside to get the mail and just pray that someone will walk by who can call them by name.

That's true for far too many people in our county and even in our church, yet this has always been true because there have always been those who find their way into isolation and don't know how to break out of it.

There was once a priest who decided that he'd go visit the entire congregation, so house by house he went, until finally he reached a place way out on the outskirts of town. The man who lived there hadn't been to the church in years. In ages. He didn't have any use for it, he said; still, the priest asked if he might just warm up by the man's fire. There, the priest moved one coal with the poker away from the rest and began asking the man questions about his wife, who had died, and his children, who had moved away. They went on talking for a while, and then the priest drew the man's attention to the coal, which had gone out having been moved away from the others, and he said, "the fire within us burns brighter when we join with the family of faith from time to time."

Reach out to someone today before the light goes out from within them, and when you do, feel the light burn a little brighter within you.

Amen.

There's a Difference Between Watching and Doing
Deuteronomy 30: 11-20 and 1st John 5: 1-6

Preached on May 9, 2021

Our second Scripture lesson is a good one for today, with today being Mother's Day, because the focus of the passage I just read is love.

That sounds nice.

Love is nice, but as every mother in here knows, love isn't just nice. When I think of love, I think not only of a mother's love portrayed in a Publix commercial. I don't just think about a warm dinner or a cup of cocoa. I think about this one afternoon when Cece was a baby. She was in a stroller, and we were walking back to Sara's parents' mountain house, when a baby bear walked by in the distance, followed by his mother, who would have mauled me had I gotten in-between her and her baby.

Love is nice, but love will kill somebody, right?

A mother's love is not just warm, wholesome, and gentle, and so when I read that word love, which occurs in our second Scripture lesson five times, I think about how love is an intense and active emotion. Love is a verb, and there's a difference between talking about love and really loving. That's why I titled this sermon: There's a Difference Between Watching and Doing.

We've been watching so much lately, confined to our houses.

How would we have made it through this pandemic without TVs and computers?

However, love calls us to do.

Love calls us to fight.

We have to remember that, especially as Christians.

I once heard a story about a Sunday school teacher who was giving her young students a tour of the church, and before they went into the worship space, she let them know how she expected them to behave. You can imagine that at their church it was something like our Sanctuary, a place to be entered with reverence and respect, therefore, before they went in, she asked her students to be quiet and to walk slowly.

"You know why we must be quiet and must walk slowly when we're in the Sanctuary, right kids?" she asked.

One of them, maybe seven years old, says, "Yes ma'am. We must be quiet in the Sanctuary so we don't wake up all the people who are sleeping."

That happens.

I admire most those who preach briefly, eloquently, and passionately. I subscribe to the preaching philosophy of Charlie Chaplain, the comedian, who once advised preachers to begin their sermons with a good joke and wrap up with a really strong ending, and those two parts (the joke and the ending) should be as close together as possible.

That's good advice.

When it comes to preaching, though, I also subscribe to the thoughts of the great Danish philosopher **Søren Kierkegaard**, who famously compared the worship space to the theater, and the preacher, not to an actor, but to a director. Kierkegaard wrote that the sanctuary and the theater look alike. Both rooms have a place for the director, a place for the actors, and a place for the audience. In the theater, the director is backstage, the actors are on stage, and the audience is in the rows of seats where they are hopefully well-entertained.

Here's the difference.

The worship space is different in the sense that the audience is always God.

Think about that for just a moment.

The audience is God. I'm one of your directors. Up here, we are the ones who tell you when to stand, what to do, and try to inspire your worshipful thoughts, and this must always be absolutely clear: while you are sitting in the pews, you are not here to be entertained because this is a place of worship. What we do in here is offer praise to the Creator, Redeemer, and Sustainer of this world.

Have you ever thought about it like that?

The question is not just whether or not you get anything out of the service. The question is: what did you give? What did you offer God? There's a difference between watching and doing, both in worship and in life.

Something I'll always remember is how years ago, I was in Tim Hammond and Jimmy Scarr's Sunday school class, and Tim told us that he doesn't watch movies because he doesn't like to watch other people live their lives; he'd rather be out in the world living his own.

I like that because it's true.

I am not a passive observer but an actor on the earth, and before my short time here is over, I've been called on to play my part, to run my race, to glorify God and enjoy Him forever, to love God and obey His commandments. In addition to our two lessons for today, Scripture is clear on this point in several places.

From the book of James, we are warned: don't be hearers of the Word, but doers.

Moses warns us not to just memorize the Ten Commandments or notice when your friends violate them but follow them yourself for your own good. In so doing, you choose life.

The author of 1st John is adamant on this point. Just two weeks ago, we read: "Little children, let us love, not in word or speech, but in truth and action." That's a good, clear, sound, and transparent admonition, which reminds us that Christianity is not a spectator sport, but a way of life marked by faith, hope, and the greatest of these, love. That's the truth, and that makes us different from all the spectators around us, who are busy watching rather than doing. Being different from all of them is OK because loving also requires distinctiveness.

Now, not everyone wants to be distinctive.

I haven't always wanted to be.

I remember being in sixth grade and wanting more than anything else in the world to be just like everyone else, to avoid being distinctive. I don't think I had any opinions of my own. I don't know what kind of shoes I actually liked. I just wanted the kind of shoes that everyone else had, even though they cost about $125. I remember asking my mom to buy them for me. She wouldn't and probably said something like, "Joe, don't you know that you don't need those shoes to be special. You're so special just as you are."

That's love talking, and maybe love won't get you through sixth grade, but it will get you through life. In this life, we cannot be afraid of what makes us distinctive. You may know already that the word *distinctive* is the key word Jeff Bezos used in his most recent letter delivered to *Amazon* shareholders. He said that there are all these pressures to conform to this world, and conforming, while it might make life temporarily easier and less conflictual, it actually leads to death.

Quoting a book called *The Blind Watchmaker* by Richard Dawkins, Bezos reminds us that:

Staving off death is a thing that you have to work at. Left to itself the body tends to revert to a state of equilibrium with its environment. Our bodies, for instance, are usually hotter than our surroundings, and in cold climates they have to work hard to maintain the differential. When we die the work stops, the temperature differential starts to disappear, and we end up the same temperature as our surroundings.

This is a powerful quote, and I'm thankful that Dr. Jeffrey Meeks emailed me the article about Bezos where it's quoted because it points to our Christian calling, which is to be set apart, to be distinctive, to be citizens of the Kingdom of Heaven, even while living in established countries on the earth. The only way we'll be able to do it is if we know so well that we are loved and accepted by God that we stop working so hard to be loved and accepted by the world.

Right now, the Church is getting all torn up again about who is in and who is out. Who can be loved, and who can't be? In the *Marietta Daily Journal*, I read about a preacher who spoke right to his son before the congregation during the worship service, "Son, I want you to know that your father wouldn't kiss the bishop's ring or kneel to the liberal theology sweeping this denomination, which is really no theology at all."

He said this to his son to thunderous applause, and it made me very afraid and worried because the most loving things are done when God is the only One there to applaud.

Love so often comes without an obvious reward.

Just yesterday, I heard a sermon about that from Rev. Chelsea Waite, who is one of the pastors at Ebenezer Baptist Church. She told a story about a ten-year-old boy whose mother asked him to do some chores around the house, even though he really didn't want to do them. Finally, she said, "I'm going for a walk, and when I get back, they had better be done." Well, she walked back in the house, and they were. The whole house was clean, but there was a note on the counter, which turned out to be a bill:

Took out the trash - $5.00.

Cleaned the windows - $25.00.

Vacuumed the kitchen - $10.00.

Scrubbed the toilets - $35.00.

The total came in to $75.00, which this mother wasn't going to pay. Instead, she wrote a bill of her own to her son:

Carried you around in my womb for 40 weeks – free.

Labored for 5 hours – free.

Changed all your diapers – free.

Fed you, soothed you, even in the middle of the night – free.

This is what love is. Love is active. It is doing, not watching, and so often it is done without celebration or applause. Mothers know that, perhaps better than anyone.

Fathers are still learning it.

I started picking up our girls from school on Wednesdays, and for the first two times, I couldn't remember to bring my carpool numbers. When I finally got it right with my carpool numbers proudly displayed, I pointed them out to Ms. Williams who runs the pick-up line and who is the twin sister of Stacy Jenson, one of our newest members. I was expecting her to applaud me for having shown up well-prepared; instead, she said to me, "What do you want, a parade for doing the minimum of what's required?" Actually, I do because some of us want a parade, but mothers know that love doesn't often get you a parade, and most of the time, love requires sacrifice instead, which is much more likethe love of God than anything else.

The Lord, Who sacrificed everything for us, His love looks like a mother's love in the sense that to love a child, you have to allow a part of yourself, or maybe several parts, to die.

You have to let your independence die because a little child is completely dependent on you. You have to let your freedom die because you aren't free.

Everywhere you go, your heart is tied to someone else.

You have to let your privacy die because you can't even use the bathroom alone if there's newborn in the house. Even today, my children are still doing that. Both of them walked in on me when I was in the shower yesterday, and a little part of my dignity died, and their eyes are still burning. Still, in part, that's what love is, and so those who don't know much about it aren't dying necessarily but that hardly means they're living.

In this terribly superficial and divided world where it can be so difficult to know what to do and what to say and where it becomes so easy just to conform, I realize that the love our second Scripture lesson calls us to is an active and risky thing: "By this we know that we love the children of God, when we love God and obey His commandments." As you think about that verse, think about how loving feels, and the next time you are faced with a choice between staying quiet and safe or speaking the truth of your heart, you'll know exactly what you should do.

I remember those times I listened to love and risked something.

It was scary, but love is scary.

It's the difference between doing what is easy and doing what is right.

It's the difference between doing what is popular and what is true.

It's the difference between slowly dying and really living.

It's the difference between watching and doing what we are called to do as His disciples.

On this Mother's Day, think about those women who have loved you, and don't just think of their hugs. Think about their terribly dangerous and sacrificial love and go and do likewise.

Amen.

The Next Book
Ephesians 1: 15-23 and Acts 1: 1-11
Preached on May 16, 2021

Today, we honor graduates of high school and college, and we have an eerily appropriate pair of Scripture lessons for the occasion, for today is what the Church calls Ascension Sunday, when we celebrate that moment when the Lord Jesus Christ ascended into Heaven, and the disciples stood and watched, staring off into the sky even after He was gone from their sights. I think about those disciples today in light of what graduation means, and I think about how maybe they were realizing that, for the first time, they were really left all on their own.

That's a significant feeling, realizing that you're all on your own.

Some people feel that, and it makes them excited, but I doubt the first disciples were excited. I suspect they were terrified. I imagine that what the disciples were feeling was something like what I was feeling when my mom dropped me off at college.

That day, my mom helped me get moved in, she attended a few of the orientation meetings, and then, over lunch, she said, "Well, I'm about to start crying, and once I start, I'm not sure I'm going to stop, so I'm leaving. I love you so much. Bye." Then she gave me a hug and left. I remember watching her walk away. It was an eerie feeling. She was gone, and this was back in the old days before cell phones, so she really was gone, headed back to Marietta, Georgia while I stayed in Clinton, South Carolina, left up to my own devices.

Among other things, that afternoon I set up the answering machine in the dorm room (that tells you about how old I am). Jesus leaving the disciples was something like that. Maybe you've heard of helicopter parents, who sort of hover around even after their kids go off to school. Jesus lifted from the earth, He was airborne, Scripture tells us, but He really left, so the disciples truly were back on the earth trying to figure out how to keep the Church going without Him.

Do you have any idea what that would have felt like?

Some people don't, though I imagine most people do, and having had that feeling several times myself, I want to stay in that feeling for a moment to really think about it and to compare the feeling those disciples must have felt with what growing up and becoming an adult is like. What I know that every parent wants is to prepare their kids for life so that they can get along on their own. Many parents question how successful they've been at doing so, but parents, compare yourself to Jesus for a moment. No one can do better than Jesus at anything, and when Jesus left, were the disciples really prepared?

Do they seem ready?

Are they anxious to spread their wings?

How responsible do they really appear to be?

I remember well enough how prepared I was for college. Honestly, I was not prepared much at all. Having really focused my schedule to do as little academically as possible during my last semesters of high school, on my first days of college, we took a few tests as a part of freshman orientation, and I tested right into remedial English. Apparently, shop and weight training weren't the classes I should have been focusing on in high school because this wasn't English 101 that I tested into. I wasn't ready for that. I tested into this class that was something like "learning English as a second language," and our professor was helping us with comma placement and when to preface a noun with "a" or "an."

In addition to my weak English skills, I had never written a check.

I had never done my own laundry.

I had never taken a car to the mechanic.

I had never been arrested, either, but soon enough, I learned more or less what that was all about. My point here is this: even the disciples don't seem particularly prepared. Jesus leaves, and they don't know what to do without Him. They're just standing there looking up at the sky, and so parents, you have to say to yourself in these last few weeks before your chicks leave the nest, "If Jesus couldn't get the disciples ready for life on their own, I need to cut myself some slack." It's impossible to completely prepare a person for independence because there are some things in life that you won't ever learn how to do until you have to do them on your own.

Do you know the hymn *Jesus Walked This Lonesome Valley*?

It goes like this:

Jesus walked this lonesome valley;

He had to walk it by himself.

Oh, nobody else could walk it for him;

He had to walk it by himself.

And then it goes:

You must go and stand your trial;

You have to stand it by yourself.

Oh, nobody else can stand it for you;

You have to stand it by yourself.

That's right, and in doing so, you'll find the strength that you didn't know you had.

You'll learn to rely on a Power that you never knew was there.

You'll begin to walk on your own.

You'll run, without waiting for someone else to lead the way.

Once Jesus ascends into Heaven, the final lesson can be taught, and the final preparation is complete because the disciples are now having to do what Jesus had been doing for them.

Dr. Martin Luther King Jr. tells his version of this same story in one of his sermons. He was in Birmingham, which you might know was such a violent place during the Civil Rights Movement that some folks called it "Bombingham." Dr. King's life was threatened while he was there. He was in danger, and he couldn't sleep. The thought of that brick that had been thrown through a window of the house he was staying in kept him up. He knew that not only was his life at risk, but that of his wife and children as well, who were staying in the house with him.

Sleep alluding him, he went into the kitchen, made himself a cup of coffee, and there he thought about how much he wanted to talk with his father, who was miles away back home in Atlanta. He couldn't depend on his father for comfort in this moment because his father was too far away, but in this moment of realizing how far away his father was, he bowed his head in prayer and he asked God for help, and he felt as though he was possibly doing this for the first time all on his own.

Now, I don't think that Dr. King meant this is the first time he had ever prayed. I feel sure that he had prayed plenty of times before; however, you don't know that you've been leaning on your parent's faith or your grandparent's faith until you're bowing your head before Almighty God in a state of deep, personal need. The old preachers used to say that God has plenty of children, but he doesn't have any grandchildren because just being related to someone who has faith isn't enough. You can't inherit faith, you have to have your own, and so being in the proximity of the Miracle Worker isn't enough to prepare the disciples for what they must do. Being the son or daughter of a preacher, Sunday school teacher, or a missionary isn't enough.

Life doesn't always care who you're related to. Your bloodline isn't going to get you into the Kingdom of God; you've got to walk that lonesome valley on your own.

You've got to walk it by yourself.

Nobody else can walk it for you.

Nobody else can study for you.

Nobody else can take the test for you, either.

Think about what's happened when parents have tried.

You've heard about the testing scandals.

Our girls have been watching *Full House* reruns, and all I can think about when I see Aunt Becky is how she helped her kids cheat on the SAT. Come on, Aunt Becky. You can't do that because not only will they get caught, you're also preparing them to fail at life.

Now listen, I've had a lot of growing up to do.

There was a time when I absolutely could not force myself to maintain my automobile. I was 21 years old and thought I was too busy to get the car fixed, especially because I had to get together with my friends from college for the weekend in Charleston. I left late at night, and somewhere in-between Columbia and Charleston, the transmission started smoking. It was late, I was in the middle of nowhere, and the car quit on me.

It just gave out.

I made it to the shoulder and cut the engine, then tried to crank it again, hoping it had reset or something. It hadn't. What do you do next? This was in those days before there were cell phones, it was dark out, my car broke down, and I had on cowboy boots.

What do you do in a situation like that one?

You start walking.

Because nobody else is walking for you.

After four miles I made it to an exit that had a pay phone.

I called a wrecker and asked the dispatcher if the wrecker could pick me up at the exit before picking up the car. She said, "Sir, it's a tow truck, not a taxicab." I'll remember that line for the rest of my life, but that night I learned a lesson the hard way because sometimes that's the only way thick-headed people ever learn.

Didn't Jesus tell them what they should do?

Didn't He?

Hadn't He already told Peter?

Hadn't He already taught Thomas?

Hadn't He already showed them all?

Still, the only way they're going to do it on their own is if He leaves them behind.

Now, I don't think Jesus wanted to leave them any more than my mother wanted to leave me at college, but she loved me too much not to help me learn that most important lesson, and in leaving me, one chapter of my life came to an end. Just when that chapter ended, another one began. That's maybe the most important thing to remember: the main character, the one everyone else depended on, leaves while the story keeps going.

Our second Scripture lesson began: "In the first book, Theophilus, I wrote about all that Jesus did and taught." You might know that the author of the book of Acts is also the author of the Gospel of Luke. In the first book, the author wrote to his friend Theophilus to tell him "all that Jesus did and taught." Acts is the next book, and just because Jesus leaves, that doesn't mean the story ends.

It means a new chapter is beginning.

For many of you, this month is full of celebrations to mark the end of the first book. In the midst of all that celebration, give thanks to God and be ready for the beginning of the next one, where you are the main character. As this next book begins, don't be afraid. Keep walking and remember always who you are and remember always Who is with you, even if you can't see Him.

You are God's own at the beginning of a new story.

Amen.

Too Light a Thing
Isaiah 49: 1-7 and Acts 2: 1-21

Preached on May 23, 2021

The week before last, I had an incredible opportunity. It was career day at the Marietta Center for Advanced Academics, and I was one of the featured guests. Honored to have a table right beside Dr. Bob Harper and his daughter Mandy, who were there to tell those kids what being a dermatologist is all about, I laid out my Greek and Hebrew Bibles and my preaching robe, prepared to inspire some 5th graders to become pastors. Interestingly, I think that examining moles and protecting people from skin cancer made a lot more sense to most of those kids than anything I had to say.

One of those kids saw my robe and thought I dressed up like *Harry Potter* for a living. Noticing how many kids were confused by my vocation, about half-way through the morning, Bob asked if the kids had asked me any interesting questions, and they had.

"Have you really married people?" one wanted to know.

"Yes, I have."

"Have you ever cried at a funeral?"

"Absolutely."

The most interesting, though, was asked in just the faintest whisper: "How likely is it that someone could be possessed by a demon?"

That was a hard question to answer.

I told her it was very rare, though if she wanted to talk more about it, she should give me a call, and I gave her a business card, which felt like a cold response, but I'm not used to being asked that kind of question. Presbyterians don't often talk about such things. Among the Christian denominations, we're sometimes called the "frozen chosen."

We don't talk much about hell or demons.

We don't often clap, either.

We rarely lift our hands in praise.

We tend to be so science-led and rationally minded that we leave things like exorcisms and snake handling to those who speak in tongues.

I've heard a woman speak in tongues only once. We were both chaplains at the Metro State Women's Prison, and the Holy Spirit fell upon her, and she began to prophecy. For me, this was an otherworldly experience. As a white, Southern, college-educated Presbyterian, speaking in tongues is not in the repertoire; however, speaking in tongues is neither foreign to Scripture nor to the Christian tradition, so today we celebrate it a little bit. Today is called Pentecost Sunday, which is a lesser-known holiday. Earlier this week, my wife, Sara, asked me if we were going to sing more hymns nobody knows. Yes, we are. The Pentecost hymns aren't as popular as Christmas carols, but we still have to sing them.

This is the second Sunday in a row where the Church celebrates a less-popular holiday. Last Sunday, we celebrated Ascension Sunday, the day when we consider that line from the Apostles' Creed: "the third day he rose again from the dead; he ascended into Heaven," and today we celebrate the gift of the Holy Spirit given to the disciples not long after Jesus ascended. It's called Pentecost, and it's worth celebrating, too.

Today, we read in the second chapter of the book of Acts:

They were all together in one place, and suddenly from heaven there came a sound like the rush of a violent wind, and it filled the entire house where they were sitting. Divided tongues, as of fire, appeared among them, and a tongue rested on each of them. All of them were filled with the Holy Spirit and began to speak in other languages, as the Spirit gave them ability.

Can you imagine?

That's what today is all about.

This momentous event.

It's a day worth celebrating, but that doesn't mean it's familiar or understood, for while there are plenty of Christmas movies on the Hallmark Channel, no one is making any Pentecost movies. I can imagine why that is, but our brothers and sisters in the Pentecostal Churches would love a few good Hallmark movies about Pentecost, so I've been kicking some ideas around. Imagine a movie with a plot like this:

- An old man gets his house cleaned every day by a woman who speaks only Spanish. They can't understand each other, but then one day the Spirit comes, and he can speak so that she can understand. They fall in love and live happily ever after.

- Or a dad has trouble connecting with his preteen daughter. He tries to sound cool, saying things he's heard her say to her friends, like "pop-off" and "yeet" but it doesn't work until the miracle happens, and suddenly all her daughter hears is how much her dad loves her.

I could keep going with these movie ideas. I have more; however, this is what I want to emphasize. What we're celebrating today is not only that the disciples are suddenly able to speak in languages they didn't know before. That's part of it. The other part is that the crowds there could understand.

In the words of Rev. Anna George Traynham of Shallowford Presbyterian Church in Atlanta: *the miracle isn't that people spoke. People speak all the time. The miracle of Pentecost is that people were understanding each other.*

That's truly a miracle.

These disciples had been all together in one place.

The Spirit came, and they were all given this incredible gift, but the gift didn't just enable them to speak in languages they'd never spoken in before. They were speaking, and the crowds were understanding. It's there in verses five and six: "Now there were devout Jews from every nation under heaven living in Jerusalem. And at this sound the crowd gathered and was bewildered, because each one heard them speaking in the native language of each."

It's not just that the disciples could speak, it's that others were able to understand, so I ask you, shouldn't we spend more time thinking about Pentecost, for how many among us are capable of speaking and being truly understood?

Not that many, which is why Pentecost is different.

How many out in the world have something to say? How many puff themselves up with their proud opinions? Who get on their soapboxes and spout off at any captive audience?

Plenty do, while Pentecost is different because the Spirit enabled these disciples to speak in a language that the nations of the world made sense of.

Now, back to Career Day at our daughter's school.

As I said, there were kids there who didn't know anything about being a preacher, and a lot of them were a little wary of me once they found out who I am and what I do, so I had some free time. Fortunately, also with me on Career Day at Cece's school was Roy Vanderslice's daughter Rebecca. Roy and his wife, Joan, are longtime members here. Rebecca and I were talking about her dad, who will not only invite you to ride in his Tesla, he's also a language student. Knowing that, I showed Rebecca this app on my phone that's helping me to learn Spanish, and I suggested she get that for her dad for Christmas or something. She told me that he wouldn't want it because he doesn't really want to learn another language. He just wants to know four or five words in all the languages. When he meets someone, he wants to be able to say, "please," "thank you," and "nice to meet you," in the languages that they speak.

Can you believe how beautiful that is?

That's a slice of Pentecost.

The disciples spoke in a way that each person understood.

People were so honored that God would go this far to speak to them in their mother tongues that they stopped and listened.

That's the miracle of today, and it's a miracle that matters in a world where so many keep talking while their words fall on deaf ears.

How often has it been this way with you?

You spoke without fully appreciating who you were speaking with.

You were talking, but there was no understanding.

It happened once with me while I was in handcuffs.

Last Sunday, I alluded to having been arrested as a college student. That's sort of true. What happened is I got in a little bit of trouble with the campus police for climbing into a condemned building on campus. Then, by the school paper, I was assigned to interview one of the officers who caught me, and for the picture, I asked him to put me in handcuffs. I thought it would make a neat action shot. The trouble was that he'd used the handcuffs so seldom that he didn't have the key. After someone took the picture, for hours I was in the handcuffs as he looked around the public safety office for the key. Then he thought maybe he had left the key at home, so he drove me there in the squad car, and this was the weirdest thing (Yes, it got even weirder.). It was when we got to his house that I really learned who this man was. Every wall of his house it seemed like was covered in certificates of recognition for his public service. Every wall, certificate after certificate, "with appreciation," "in celebration of," "with honor and distinction." I tried to read them all while he looked for that key, which he never found.

He never found the key, and eventually, a locksmith had to cut the handcuffs off of me.

I remember it like it was yesterday, not just being cut out of handcuffs, but that I had been writing about this man without really understanding who this man was, and it basically took a miracle for me to get it.

That's Pentecost.

It's a holiday we need to celebrate, for how often do we fail to understand each other?

How often in this world do we fail to understand what it's like to be a police officer?

I tell you; our country's lack of full understanding doesn't stop people from talking.

Some criticize the police without understanding how hard their jobs are.

Far too many talk about race without any knowledge of what it still means to be Black in America.

Some think they know.

They really think they know, so they talk, but as they talk, the divide gets wider because they speak without understanding.

What does the Spirit do, though?

He gave the disciples the words, the words that the world could understand, which is absolutely a miracle that our society needs today. Just think about what's happening in school boards across our state. Maybe you've read about it. Crowds of angry parents show up to talk over each other. If you don't say what one wants to hear, he'll shout you down without taking the time to listen. It sounds like life as usual in our world today. Meanwhile, there are little girls in our schools who are wondering how common it is to be possessed by a demon.

What Pentecost reminds us is that communication, real communication, requires love.

That's what happened so long ago. These disciples weren't talking so that they could advance their own agendas.

These disciples were up there trying to communicate to the world how much love God has for every person on the Earth, and when I say every one, that's what I mean: salvation to the ends of the earth, only let it start in our own homes.

Celebrate Pentecost and dare to try and understand your spouse.

Dare to love her well enough to really listen.

Dare to lovingly speak to the police officer who is a human, too.

Dare to acknowledge the racism that still surrounds us.

Dare to speak of love so that the walls that divide our world might come tumbling down.

Dare to believe that the salvation of this church is too light a thing and that the Spirit calls us to the 800,000 out in Cobb County, half of whom have yet to understand the love of God.

Be slow to speak.

Be ready to listen.

Work to understand.

And may your words be always abounding in steadfast love.

Amen.

www.ingramcontent.com/pod-product-compliance
Lightning Source LLC
Chambersburg PA
CBHW071431070526
44578CB00001B/71